Otherwise I Forget

A Novel

World Writing in French
A Winthrop-King Institute Series

Series Editors
Charles Forsdick (University of Liverpool)
and
Martin Munro (Florida State University)

Advisory Board Members
Jennifer Boum Make (Georgetown University)
Michelle Bumatay (Florida State University)
William Cloonan (Florida State University)
Michaël Ferrier (Chuo University)
Michaela Hulstyn (Stanford Univesity)
Khalid Lyamlahy (University of Chicago)
Helen Vassallo (University of Exeter)

There is a growing interest among Anglophone readers in literature in translation, including contemporary writing in French in its richness and diversity. The aim of this new series is to publish cutting-edge contemporary French-language fiction, travel writing, essays and other prose works translated for an English-speaking audience. Works selected will reflect the diversity, dynamism, originality, and relevance of new and recent writing in French from across the archipelagoes – literal and figurative – of the French-speaking world. The series will function as a vital reference point in the area of contemporary French-language prose in English translation. It will draw on the expertise of its editors and advisory board to seek out and make available for English-language readers a broad range of exciting new work originally published in French. This series is published in partnership with the Winthrop-King Institute, Florida State University.

Clémentine Mélois

Otherwise I Forget

A Novel

Translated by Terry Bradford

Liverpool University Press

First published in English translation by Liverpool University Press 2023
Liverpool University Press
4 Cambridge Street
Liverpool
L69 7ZU

Otherwise I Forget was first published in French as *Sinon j'oublie*
© Éditions Grasset & Fasquelle, 2017

Copyright © Clémentine Mélois, 2017
English translation copyright © Terry Bradford, 2023

The right of Clémentine Mélois to be identified as the author of this work and
Terry Bradford to be identified as translator of this work has been asserted by them
in accordance with the Copyright, Designs and Patents Act 1988.

British Library Cataloguing-in-Publication data
A British Library CIP record is available

ISBN 978-1-80207-872-5 hardback
ISBN 978-1-80207-873-2 paperback

Typeset by Carnegie Book Production, Lancaster
Printed and bound by CPI Group (UK) Ltd, Croydon CR0 4YY

Acknowledgements

All images reproduced by kind permission of Editions Grasset and Editions Fasquelle: I thank Heidi Warneke and Christiaan van Raaijen for their kind collaboration. I am also greatly indebted to Chloe Johnson of LUP for her patience and support throughout the process of readying this book for publication. The same gratitude I owe to Rebecca Spence and Alwyn Harrison. Finally, thanks to Clémentine Mélois herself: for her trust and time spent helping me with my own list of queries.

Terry Bradford

TABLE OF CONTENTS

On this earth, there are two types of people: those who throw stuff away and those who keep stuff. And it runs in the family.

When I was a kid, the *best* Sundays were those when we went on trips to the local rubbish tip (the Land of Muck and Money). Back then, out in the countryside, you could still find fragments of lives unknown, jumbled together as if in the wake of some catastrophe, thrown on the scrapheap, abandoned. We were on a mission: we were looking for enamel buckets, which my father would take as the raw material for his sculptures. But we also found dolls whose hair was not burnt *too* much, goatskin leather jackets, cobbled shoes, and a whole host of relics and scrap metal, which we would hold aloft like trophies before they were ensconced in the back of our old Citroen van. Quite simply, we gave these things a new life. Not only did these forays afford us the pleasure of discovery – they gave us a vague but pleasurable feeling of breaking the rules, of swimming against the current, of sticking two fingers up to 'respectable' folk. What other people threw away, we turned into treasure.

Rubbish tips like that have long since disappeared, but more fragile fragments of the lives of others can still be found, today, on the streets where we live. You just have to keep your eyes open and look at the ground when you're walking around. The little scraps of paper we see lying there are often shopping lists. No one wants them – all you have to do is bend down and pick them up. And just as there are hotspots for finding wild mushrooms, so there are hotspots for such lists. Of course, you'd expect to find them around supermarkets, but you can find them anywhere – in fact, the best finds are those that are most unexpected.

I like lists and I like what they can teach me about people's inner selves – there's a hint of voyeurism in this, tempered by their anonymity. Everyone – or pretty much so – *writes* lists, and writing is the precise subject that this collection deals with throughout. Writing so as not to forget, writing without checking oneself, with no frills, as if inside oneself, writing what we really need.

Shopping lists – like a private diary – are not intended to be read by other people. They reveal people's obsessions, their habits, their character, their handwriting, and spelling. And yet they are thrown away without a second thought (being biodegradable), and so are exposed with no modesty to the eyes of others. Who's interested in a scrap of paper lying on the ground? It's of no interest whatsoever. And yet …

Whenever I find one, I say to myself, 'Aha! I don't have that one!' Like a child might exclaim when they open a new packet of Panini football stickers for their collection. Then I engage in a parody of an investigation to try to work out who's hiding behind this writing. Is it a man or a woman? This guy's on a diet, she's going to bake a cake – maybe she has guests? This person's cat is spoilt rotten, he's obsessive, she's a scatterbrain, how old are they?

The study that I undertake is but a fiction, a game. I'm telling stories to myself. But the poetry emanating from these lists is quite real. These writings have much to say about our everyday habits, our obsessions, our past, and our little quirks. They capture a truth that gets to me.

From my collection (stored in a number of shoe boxes), I have selected ninety-nine lists. Each one was written by someone – whether male or female – whose life, concerns, and way of using language I have imagined. Together they form the characters of this book – these stories are their portraits.

How should we take account of, question, describe what happens every day and recurs every day: the banal, the quotidian, the obvious, the common, the ordinary, the infra-ordinary, the background noise, the habitual?

Georges Perec, *The Infra-ordinary*[1]

1   Georges Perec, *Species of Spaces and Other Pieces*, ed. and trans. John Sturrock (London: Penguin, 1997), p. 206.

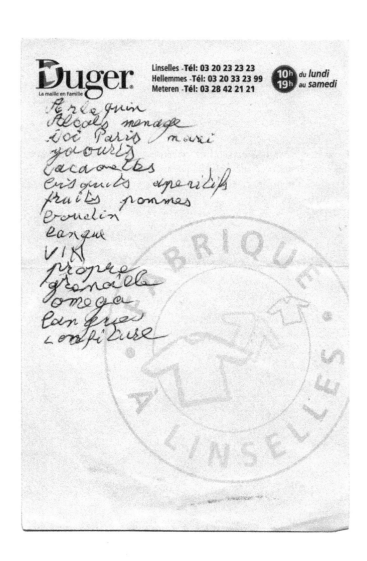

Duger.
La maille en Famille

Linselles -**Tél: 03 20 23 23 23**
Hellemmes -**Tél: 03 20 33 23 99**
Meteren -**Tél: 03 28 42 21 21**

10h du *lundi*
19h au *samedi*

Arlequin • Surjical spirits • Ici Paris maxi • yoghurts • peenuts
nibbles • fruit apples • black pudding • tongue • WINE
clean • new potato • omega • tongue • jam

• 4 •

Pierrette

The other day, me and Pierrot went to Unico. We like to get there early, to Unico, before they open, around 9 a.m., to beat the crowds. But this time, we were there too early, and we had to sit waiting in the car until they opened. It's better to get there early. Especially if you're wanting to buy meat. I know the butcher at Unico – a young lad ... he was with Isabelle for a while, but that's over now. When I've got guests, and I'm wanting a joint or a roast of beef to feed eight, for example, he always gives me the best cuts. And he always calls me, 'Young Lady'! He says, 'Here's your roast beef, Young Lady'. I'm not going to contradict him!

Anyway, so, the other day, we were sat in the car, waiting for Unico to open, and I heard something like the sound of a mosquito, but I didn't see it! I told Pierrot, but could we swat it!? Not a chance – we couldn't even see it, the damn mosquito. And ever since, I've been scratching! Scratching I've been! Anyway! You can say what you like, when it comes to Unico, you're better off getting there early.

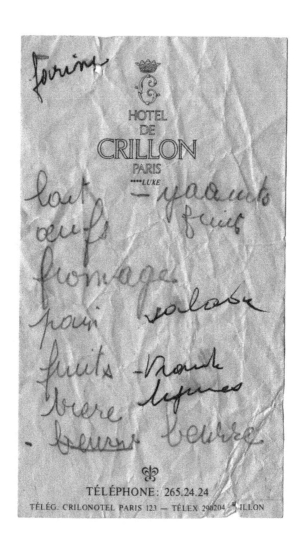

HOTEL
DE
CRILLON
PARIS
****LUXE

TÉLÉPHONE: 265.24.24
TÉLÉG. CRILONOTEL PARIS 123 — TÉLEX 290204 ＊ＮILLON

*flour • milk • fruit yoghurts • eggs • cheese • bread • salad • fruit
meat • veg • beer • ~~butter~~ • butter*

Christophe

The French Happiness Index. Come on, *really?* The idea of measuring a nation's well-being in terms of their economic activity is completely bloody stupid. As if the fact that you're consuming stuff meant you were in a good mood. 'Life's all good, I've got a new car!' Well, I've got a new car with all the extras, and life's not good at all. I know I'm being simplistic, but I can't help but be riled by their turns of phrase. Dammit! To hell with your sustainable development indicators and your growth rates. I've got a Gold Card and I'll bloody well be unhappy if I want to be.

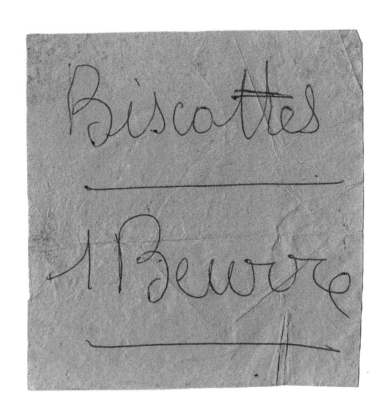

Biscottes • 1 Butter

Élodie

I've forgotten the name of the film I saw on the telly, the other evening – maybe *Between Love and Hate,* or something like that. It was rubbish, but it took my mind off things. It was set in sunny Florida. There was this really good-looking guy, Brian, with dark hair and a strong jawline, and he had a cleft in his chin like Michael Jackson had done – he was a single dad because he'd lost his wife in an accident when she was very young. He met this bottle blonde with perfect make-up who didn't really know what she wanted to do with her life. Then all sorts of crazy, impossible things happened to them. To begin with, they hated each other, obviously. They hurled abuse at each other, but of course by the end of the film they ended up together. That sort of thing would never happen to me. And anyhow, in films like that, even when there's an explosion, their hair looks perfect, and they drive 4x4s the size of a tank, as if the cars over there ran on water. Whereas my hair – when it rains – sticks out, the Clio makes a weird noise when I change gear, and I only have to *look* at a bowl of spag bol and I end up with sauce down my trousers. It's the pits.

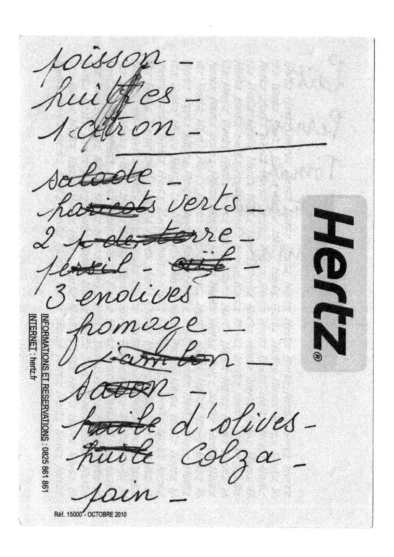

poisson -
huîtres -
1 citron -
_____

salade -
haricots verts -
2 p. de terre -
persil - ~~oié~~ -
3 endives —
fromage -
jambon -
~~daurm~~ -
huile d'olives -
huile colza -
pain -

fish • oysters • 1 lemon • salad • green beans • 2 potatoes
parsley • garlic • 3 endives • cheese • ham • soap • olive oil
rapeseed oil • bread

• 10 •

Stéphane

School's out and we're off to the States for two weeks, treating ourselves to a road trip on a Harley, *Easy Rider* style. West Coast, wide-open space, and adventure, here we come! We could try Highway 61 Revisited, from New Orleans to Chicago. We could take in Nashville, Saint-Louis, Memphis at any pace we want, and without a care in the world. We could spend the night in dodgy motels, we could eat jambalaya and alligator meat, and I could buy myself a leather jacket like the one I had when I was 16, and a bandana. After a day's riding in the blazing heat, we'll rock up – covered in dust – at some one-horse town, and we'll be welcomed with open arms, free to drink as much coffee as we want from enormous mugs. In the evening, we could go to blues bars filled only with locals and no tourists, and we might discover the most amazing groups that nobody's ever heard of, and it'll be OK to smoke inside, even if I've given up. And I'd like to have a T-bone steak and eat pancakes with syrup, and try biscuits and gravy with home-made fries. And we could make love like in *Wild at Heart*.

coke zero • juice • cucumber • sweets? • this evening …

Christel

This morning, in a fit of bravura such as I am occasionally prone to, steeled to face the terrible truth, I got on the bathroom scales. The display said: 'Low battery'. I took it quite well, I think.

So, now I've got just a few hours to buy some new batteries and lose 22 lbs.

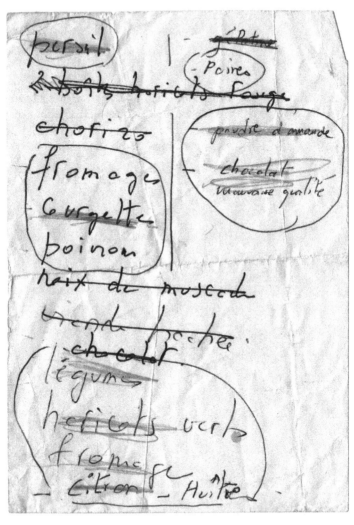

parsley • ~~gelatine~~ • pears • ~~2 tins kidney beans~~ • ~~chorizo~~
ground almond • cheese • courgettes • sweet pepper
cheap chocolate • ~~nutmeg~~ • ~~mince~~ • ~~chocolate~~
veg • green beans • cheese • lemon • Oysters

Michèle

In the past, despite everything, I would cook. When the girls were little, I used to cook things for them. Chicken, baked potatoes, or a gratin in the oven. Sometimes I'd even bake cakes. I'm not saying I enjoyed it, but I did it all the same, because it needed doing. Now I just can't do it anymore. It really gets on my tits – I mean, you wouldn't *believe* how much it gets on my tits. You have to lay the table, sit down for an hour to talk trivia, 'Ooh, what do you put in your sauce?' and all that. I couldn't give a flying fart about the sauce. And afterwards, there's all the tidying away and the washing-up that needs doing, then the drying up, putting everything back in its place, sweeping up, and bang goes half the day, wasted for nothing. Not to mention that just a few hours later, you've already got to start thinking about the evening meal. All that time *gone* … What a waste. All is vanity. My dream would be that they invent a pill to take instead of meals. You'd take your pill and hey presto! You'd not be hungry, and you could do other more interesting things, like read, go for a walk, or surf the net.

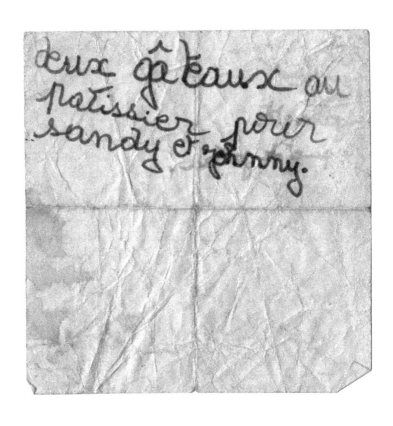

two cakes from the patisserie for sandy and johnny.

Sandy

In the sewers under Paris, there are real-life alligators, three metres long. They can come up through the toilet and bite your butt, and sometimes they can eat you all up in one go. That's why I always wait until I'm bursting, almost peeing my pants, before I go to the toilet, and I check it three times before I sit down, because last year I got bitten by Charlie, Uncle Jean's cocker spaniel. Jean said that the dog had just given me a nip, but in fact it really hurt a lot and I had a red mark on my arm, so an alligator bite must be a thousand times worse, and there's no way I want to find out for myself.

Mes Courses

Coton

Cotton

Mireille

For Monday's meeting, I'm going to stack the odds in my favour. I'll wear the most elegant clothes, but with a touch of originality: pencil skirt, halftone blouse, and – the pièce de résistance – the blazer with shoulder pads that came last week. Nude makeup, but with matte red lipstick to show that I'm a woman who dares. I'll have to remember not to smile too much, or they'll see it as a sign of weakness. As for accessories, no handbag. NEVER a handbag. That's a tip from Hillary Clinton for women who want to get to the top in politics. You need to be able to move freely, if you want to embrace people and shake hands, like male politicians do. But then where am I going to put my phone, my cash and cards, and my keys? The blazer has no pockets, and anyway that stuff would ruin the lines, and that wouldn't be elegant. In the worst-case scenario, I could maybe leave my bag at reception. I often wonder how male politicians manage this. Maybe they have an assistant who holds their stuff for them while they're busy meeting and greeting people.

2 Beer • ~~*2 P ack Beer*~~ • *endive* • *tortoise* FOOD

Jean

What I like about you, tortoise, is that you don't go around waving your arms all over the place like those bloody idiots, out there. You hold your tongue. There are no recriminations with you. You're like me – you watch the trains roll by and you keep yourself to yourself. There's a good girl. Now, come here.

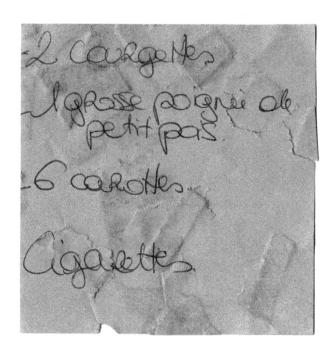

2 courgettes • 1 big handful of petits pois • 6 carrots • Cigarettes

Sandrine

I got a ticket for speeding the other day, and I tried to get the penalty points added to Olivier's license, given that he never drives. Just my luck … on the photo taken by the speed camera, you can clearly see the driver is a woman with long blonde hair. The people at the courts must've had a good laugh about that. Meanwhile, a penalty point and a 48 Euro fine, just for being 5 km/h over the limit. The Looney Left, I thank you.

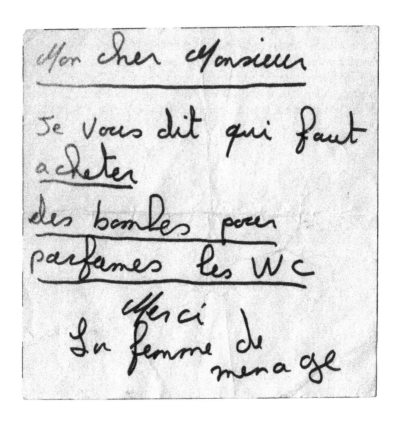

Mon cher Monsieur

Je vous dit qui faut acheter des bombes pour parfames les WC

Merci
La femme de menage

<u>Dear Sir</u> •
As I say, we need to <u>buy sum air freshener for the loos</u>
Thank you • *The cleaning lady*

Sandra

Just because they pay us 11 euros – after deductions – per hour, they think they've got the right to treat us like shit. The other day, I was just finishing mopping the floor, and the Lord of the Manor comes in with some friends. One of them made as if to take his shoes off, so as not to make a bloody great mess because it was raining out. Whereupon his Lordship says to him, 'No, really, don't worry about it … Sandra will clean up'. Well, I'll tell you this much: from now on, he can do his own cleaning. He's not a person to work for – he doesn't deserve me.

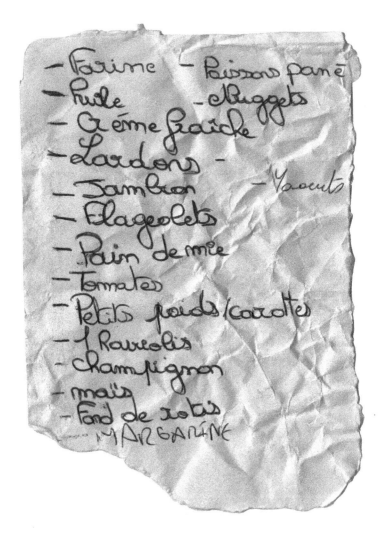

Flour • Breaded fish fillits • Nuggets • oil • Créme fraiche • Lardons
Ham • Yoghurts • Flageolet beans • Sliced loaf • Tomatoes
Petits poids/carrots • 1 Ravioli • mushroom • sweet corn
Gravy granules • MARGARINE

Océane

It's not my fault if mum's feeling lonely – I didn't ask to be born. Well, nobody did. But what she said really hurt me, and I've been feeling really guilty. And it's not as if I don't want to see her any more since I left, that's just not true. I often give her a call, and I go home practically every weekend and take my dirty washing for her to do.

La Venise Verte

Bag of sugar • cat • sausage • nut bread • mandarins
Deodorant + smell good • yoggurts • cheese • coarse salt • Koffee • minced beef
1 leek • fish-prawns •

Sylvie

We couldn't have afforded to go to Venice, so for our anniversary Philippe took me on a trip to the marshlands around Coulon, not far from Niort. It was a 5-hour drive, avoiding the motorway. When we got there, we could've spent all day watching the cows drinking from the water, and we walked barefoot through the damp grass. The next day, we went for a boat ride, and the boatman even showed us how to set fire to the water, which was fun. Everything was so calm and still, really humid, and very green. In the evening, we ended up arguing a bit, because they had coypu pâté on the menu in the restaurant. I'd spotted a coypu, that morning, in the water – they look like fat, sneaky rats. Disgusting. I told Philippe, no, never, we're not on some TV survival show, and that I'd rather die than eat rats. He had a sulk and ate his mogette beans in silence, even though I know he loves them. But later, we ended up smoothing things out and by the time we went to bed, we'd made up. Okay, so I've not been to Italy, but I reckon Coulon, the so-called Green Venice, was just as good, and at least it wasn't full of tourists.

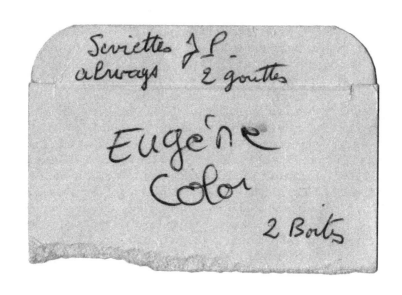

JP sanitary pads • always 2 drops • Eugène Color • 2 Boxes

Nathalie

For pity's sake, I've still not shaken off this awful mood I'm in. I feel like killing everyone. It's all down to my period, it's on its way. To make things worse, the slightest thing sets me off crying, and that's annoying. When you have a cold, everyone feels sorry for you – you get a bit of sympathy. But I can't see myself discussing my ovarian issues with my boss. Like I could really just say to him, 'I'm so sorry, Sir, I'm a bit highly strung owing to severe PMS. My breasts are terribly tender, my bra feels tight and it's really hurting. Oh, and by the way, could you *please* go easy on the aftershave? It's seriously making me queasy and I could puke at the drop of a hat'.

2 tins tuner

André

The doctor's told me I need to exercise, so I've taken his advice and every morning I exercise by walking down to the quayside to watch the guys unloading their catch. They really put their backs into it. At my time of life, you've earned the right to do diddly-squat, to don your best cap, and leave the graft to others. After I've done my exercise, I'll pop into the Maritime café for a cheeky snifter and catch up on the news.

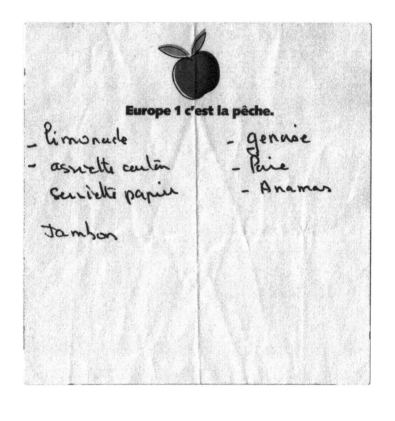

Europe 1 c'est la pêche.

- Limonade
- assiette carton
  serviette papier

Jambon

- genoise
- Poire
- Ananas

lemonade • paper plates • paper napkins • ham
spunge cake • Pear • pineapple

Steven

I'd never use Behringer gear – that sort of kit's for amateurs. The mid-bass range sounds like a horrible mush, and you can't hear yourself in the monitor. All that stuff's good for is dicking around when you're fifteen and you wanna get laid. I'm a pro, I really know my gear. When I finally get time to work on my own album, I'm gonna hire a studio, get the big guns out, go all classy, and break America. In the meantime, there's no shame in doing backing for pop stars. Everyone has to earn a crust. And many are called but few are chosen, as they say. When you're working on a job for TV or an ad, you're not there to give a YouTube tutorial, right, even if it's a good idea to fucking kill it in terms of technique. But apart from that, things ain't what they used to be when it comes to the cash side of things. I did some synching on an ad for mayonnaise, using a track from my latest EP, and the cash I got for that wasn't that much. Barely ten grand, after tax. Fuck this shit, I'm sick of it. There's really no more money in ads. It sucks.

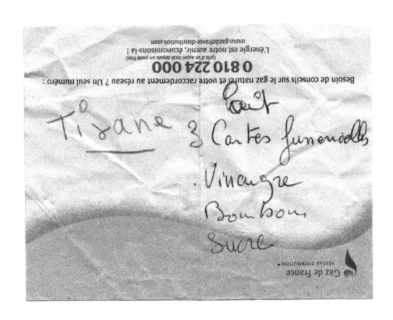

Herbal tea • milk • *3 Condolance cards* • *Vinegar* • *Sweets* • *Sugar*

Monique

Peace, at last. I'm always happy when Christmas and New Year are over – I'm always nervous beforehand. There were twelve of us in the house, including the kids, with my daughter moaning about the dog barking, her sister nagging me to buy a dishwasher, refusing to understand that they scratch the glasses, my son-in-law sat reading his newspaper in silence with a face on him as long as the day, kids being spoilt rotten and throwing tantrums, Michel wanting to stick to his usual routine, expecting us to eat at 7 on the dot when nothing's ready, and me – in the middle of all that – having to sort everything out. Not to mention the deaths. It's always during winter the oldies leave us – you'd think it was the cold and the long winter nights starting at 4 p.m. that pushes them over the edge. If I were them, I'd be the same. Even so, it don't half get to you. Three this year – and that's just since the start of December. And in the old days, they'd have a wake in the home of the departed, and you'd go and pay your respects, they'd splash some holy water around, a few words of comfort for the family, and you'd be away. Nowadays, you have to spend a whole morning driving to the arse end of nowhere to get to some characterless funeral parlour. There's nothing appealing about them whatsoever. That is, if you can talk about appeal in those circumstances.

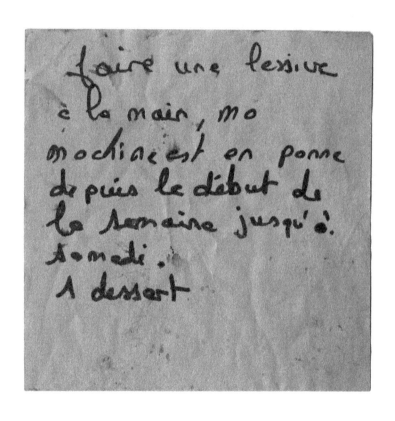

do the washing by hand – my machine's been broken since the start
of the week until Saturday • 1 dessert

Valérie

The guesthouse near Arvignac has a bridal chamber that is a-maz-ing. There's a balcony, you get breakfast, and the bedroom furniture is made from polished solid oak. There are signs for it – there's a sign on the big main road, for example, just after the waste reprocessing plant. We went to view a few others, just to get an idea – thanks, but no thanks. The rooms were tiny, and you should see the prices. The one in Arvignac has lovely gardens and the décor's gorgeous. Pink fitted carpets, Liberty curtains, place mats made from Calais lace, and full HD TV. At breakfast, there's homemade jam and they use tablecloths of real cloth – it's quality. Laurent even took a bath, and he never does that because he's usually more of a shower person. I wore my dress without sleeves, the one with the row of little buttons at the back, and we slept with the window open. It was almost as good as being on honeymoon.

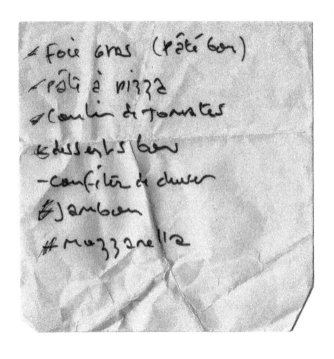

Foie gras (paté ok) • pizza base • passata • nice desserts
various jam • ham • mozzarella

Rudy

I've got to learn how to stop thinking, how to switch my brain off and pause it. It feels like it's working constantly at full pelt, like a machine on overload, like some all-invasive plant species, relentlessly shifting from one idea to the next, slowly but surely consuming all my oxygen. It's exhausting. For example, the other day, from the train, I saw a house with smoke coming from the chimney. I imagined it would be hot in there. That made me think about Canada, because it's cold over there and they need fireplaces with a chimney. Then I remembered a trip to Canada, from ages and ages ago. I was in the French-speaking region of the Laurentides, in a bar. On the TV, there was a report announcing the death of Lady Di. She was a beautiful woman who always looked sad. She led such a strange life, just to end up in a road accident in Paris – what a cruel fate. Then I wonder what make the car was. Probably a French car, maybe a Renault, or then again a Citroën. Chirac used to drive a Renault Safrane, and de Gaulle used to drive a Citroën DS. Well, they didn't drive their cars themselves, of course, because they had chauffeurs. That reminds me of my driving instructor. He would always say that when you have passengers, you should picture yourself as the driver of the Queen of England, in a Rolls Royce, driving as smoothly as possible. What was his name again? Oh yeah, Michel. He'd been in the French Foreign Legion. It must get hot in the desert, I bet you're thirsty all the time. One thing you should never do is drink your own urine – otherwise, you die. Plus, it's disgusting. Apparently, if you cut into a cactus, you can find water inside, whereas in the humps of camels – in fact – you'll find nothing but fat. There are two syllables in the word 'camel', whereas there are four in the word 'dromedary'. That's a sort of mnemonic, like the one to remember the order of the planets in the solar system: 'My Very Educated Mother Just Served Us Nine Pizzas', which gives you Mercury, Venus, Earth, Mars, Jupiter, Saturn, Uranus, Neptune, and Pluto. I really enjoyed reading Marcel Aymé's novel called *Uranus*, but I didn't enjoy the film so much – I think Gérard Depardieu was in it. These days, he owns a vineyard. And he's got very fat. If you were to cut *him* in two, would you find fat like in camels, or wine like in cacti? Well, OK, I know what I mean.

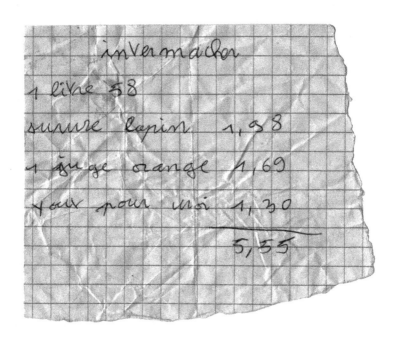

suppermarket • 1 litre 58 • wood shavins rabbit 1.98
1 orange juce 1.69 • yhurt for me 1.30 • 5.55

Didier

I do get homosexual impulsations when it comes to women. It's been more than a year since I shot my load – the last time was in 1998. I'll end up with lumps in my ball bag, I just know it.

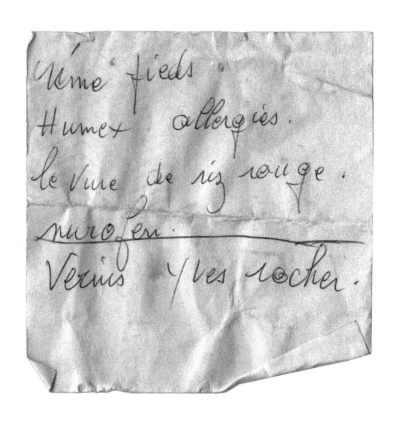

feet cream • Humex allergies • red yeast rice
<u>nurofen</u> • Nail polish yves rocher

Martine

The worst thing is the ringing in my ears. A sort of constant, high-pitched buzzing in my right ear, which has meant I'm increasingly behind with sleep and I feel completely exhausted. I can even hear the boom-boom of my heart. The homeopath reckons I'm as fit as a fiddle and just recommended I take magnesium. I think I'm going to change doctor, because this one doesn't seem to take his patients seriously. Otherwise, Chantal's sister-in-law says she knows someone who teaches yoga. She advised her to do an exercise that would be good for what I've got – it allows you to massage the inside of your own head, your jawbones, and your auditory system. It's called the lion pose, and what you have to do is stick your tongue out as far as you can down to your chin, whilst roaring like a lion and looking up to the sky at the same time. Well, what have I got to lose?

St marc toilet cleaner with neck • St Marc multi-purpose 1 1½ • vitele 2 pack • groundnut oil 3 litre • gurkhins • sider vinager 2 litre • plastic bag + punnit cakes Box • look for ~~lickure~~ liquore for maude. 2 litres lickuore for frut • butter • milk • cheese

Simone

When people my age tell me, 'Ooh, I keep falling', I turn round and say to 'em, 'Get yourself some walking poles!' And then they say, 'And what about my bag?' All you have to do is get yourself a haversack, but they turn round and say, 'Ooh, I can't do that'. And so they keep falling. I've had sticks for a good while now, me.

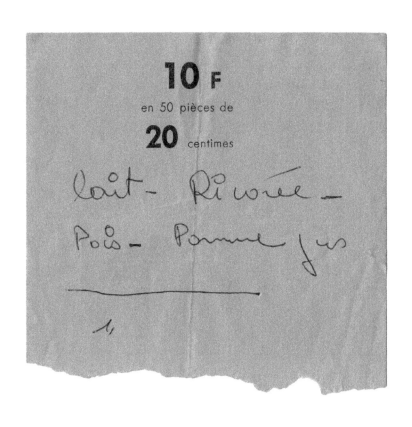

milk • Ricorée • Peas • Juice apple

Catherine

I can remember the exact moment I heard Kennedy had been assassinated. I was in a residence for young girls, in Nancy. On the day when man first walked on the moon, Barbara was two years old – she was wearing a red Raglan jumper I'd knitted for her and a pair of long stockinette shorts. My sewing machine couldn't do a zig-zag stitch, so when I put them on her, the seams came apart. When Mitterrand became president, we had a house full of people, including that photographer chap with a beard who looked like Mr Edwards from *Little House on the Prairie*. I've forgotten his name. When the Berlin Wall fell, we were watching telly – we saw Rostropovich play his cello. When Lady Di died, we'd spent the day repainting the living room. There was nothing else to do but listen to the radio while the paint dried. For the 1998 World Cup, we went to Paris one afternoon. Because they thought they were going to win, the Brazil fans were in such a frenzy that the *métro* carriage was rocking from side to side. I'd never seen anything like it. On the day of September 11, it rained, and on the morning of the *Charlie Hebdo* attacks I'd just defrosted some plums to make a tart. We lost our appetite after that.

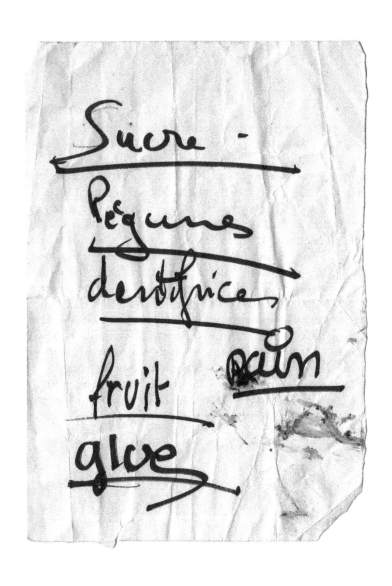

Sugar • vegetables • toothpastes • bread • fruit • glue

Kevin

They can all go fuck themselves. I'm gonna give those arseholes a piece of my mind, that'll put the wind up 'em. Oh yes, they won't look so clever then, when they realise I won't give in to their pathetic, shitty blackmail. That'll teach 'em to treat people like dirt. There's no way I'll sit back and take it, I don't give a shit – better to die on your feet than live on your knees. Down with the Establishment, fuck the police, and bye-bye bosses. If I bombed these bastards and blew their fascist heads off, the world would be a much better place. *No pasarán*, fucking bastards. I wouldn't piss on 'em if they were on fire.

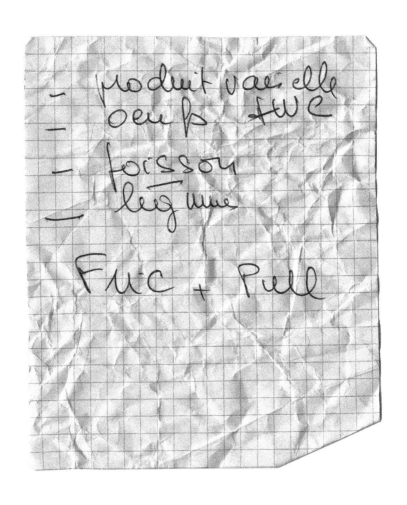

washing-up liquid • eggs + toilet • fish • vegetables • Cash + Jumper

Laura

That's the fourth person who's accused me of being a misogynist. That's way off – I've loads of female friends I get on just fine with. I just hate those women who simper and play dumb. It drives me crazy, enough to want to give them a good slap. 'I'm a girlie girl', they say as they seductively lean their head to one side ... 'I'm a girlie girl, a weak and feeble woman, and I can't possibly carry this box all on my own – my arms are like jelly, tee-hee-hee'. Stupid bitch. I just can't understand how – in the twenty-first century – anyone can conform to such archaic stereotypes. You'd think our grandmothers fought for absolutely nothing. I once heard a woman say, 'Oh, no, I'm not a feminist – I like men too much'. What's that got to do with it, for fuck's sake?

rosés

2 b d'eaux

3 ou 4 carottes

1 b de p. pois

1 p de tripes à la mode
              de caen

rosés • 2 bs of water • 3 or 4 carrots • 1 t of p. pois
1 p of caen-style tripe

Thierry

My neighbour – who teaches at a secondary school – doesn't half know a lot of stuff. He spends all his free time riding around on his bike, observing fauna and flora with a scientist's eye. One day, when he was passing a building site, he spotted a pile of cobble-stones. And there, in the middle of them, what do you think he finds? A woolly mammoth tooth. A real ancient woolly mammoth tooth that no one would've even noticed if he'd not come along. People don't know what they look like. Nor do I, but that doesn't stop me from checking every time I come across workers digging up the road, just in case. You never know … it could be worth a pretty penny.

ciment reparation
teinture grise
clous "grosse tete" =>
24 Vis reparation Sièges

cement filler • grey paint • 'big-headed' nails
24 seat fix Screws

Jérôme

I'm not the first person to come up with this, but when it comes to picking up women, you can't beat DIY shops. They're rammed with single women pulling their hair out wondering which drill to buy. They'll dither, compare, and can't decide which one to get. So I appear, like some prince charming, and offer to be their servant. Sometimes they're idiots – but not always. Women – even married women – like men who can DIY, who can reassure them, and more (if there's a connection). With a bit of skill, you can always find one who's bored with her life and wouldn't say no to a bit on the side every now and again.

dart guns • planes • batmen • pirates • catapult • swords

Oscar

I'll be the captain, and Simon's my second-in-command. Against us, there must be at least a thousand of them. They'll lay siege to the castle, but we'll hit back with our catapults, and then Simon'll get hit, but it won't be serious in the end, cos he'll get up and we'll lead the final attack with our swords. And then there'll be a mutant dragon trying to block our way, but I'll hide behind a machicolation, and thanks to my superpower I'll neutralise it, and after that we'll take back control of the castle, and people will shout hooray and thank you for saving us. It's snack time, and I hope there are some strawberry-flavoured choccy cookies left because the vanilla ones aren't nice.

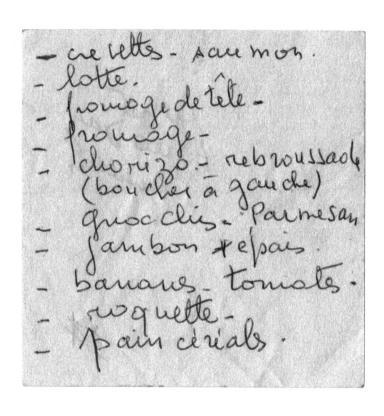

- crevettes - saumon.
- lotte.
- fromage de tête -
- fromage -
- chorizo. - rebroussade
  (boucher à gauche)
- gnocchis - Parmesan
- jambon + épais.
- bananes - tomates.
- roquette -
- pain céréals.

shrimp • salmon • monkfish • pork brawn • cheese • chorizo
double back (butcher on left) • gnocchi • Parmesan
thicker ham • bananas • tomatoes • rocket salad • multigrain cereal bread

Béatrice

There's this man dressed all in black, a bit disturbing. What's his name again? Oh, yeah – Barthes Vador, as in Roland Barthes. Anyway, in the end, this Barthes Vador turns out to be the father of the main character, a somewhat bland young man who's supposed to represent moral values. The telly guide had nothing but praise for it, but I didn't really get it.

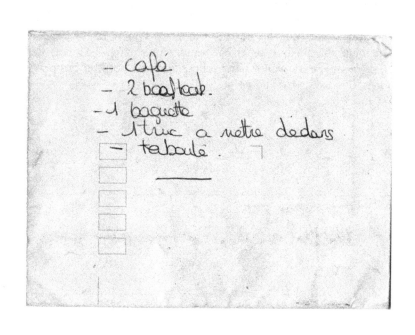

- café
- 2 beefsteak.
- 1 baguette
- 1 truc a mettre dedans
- ☐ tabboulé.
☐
☐
☐
☐
☐

coffee • 2 steaks • 1 baguette • something to put in it • taboulé

Manon

If the light turns green before I get to the end of the street, that'll mean that Mathieu is in love with me.

That one doesn't count. I walked too fast.

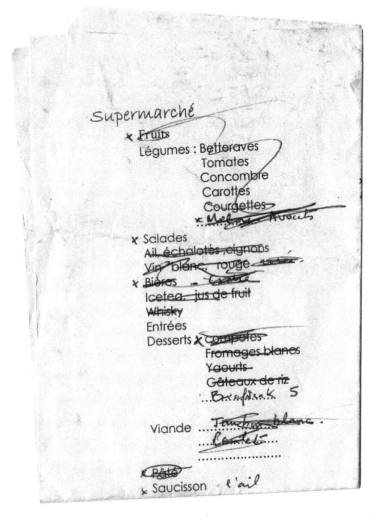

Supermarché

x Fruits
Légumes : Betteraves
Tomates
Concombre
Carottes
Courgettes
x Melons Avocats

x Salades
Ail, échalotes, oignons
Vin blanc, rouge
x Bières Cidre
Icetea, jus de fruit
Whisky
Entrées
Desserts x Compotes
Fromages blancs
Yaourts
Gâteaux de riz
... Breakfast 5

Viande .... Tour bur blanc .
.... Coulet ...
....

x Pâté
x Saucisson l'ail

*Supermarket • Fruit • Vegetables • Beetroot • Tomatoes • Cucumber
Carrots • Courgettes • Melons • Avocados • Salad • Garlic, shallots,
onions • Wine white, red, rosée • Beers • Cider • Icetea, fruit juice
Whisky • Starters • Desserts • Compotes • Fromage blanc • Yoghurts
Rice cakes • 5 steaks • Meat Cooked ham • Chicken • Pâté
Garlic sausage*

Charlène

I'm in a long corridor with closed doors on either side – it looks like the office, but not exactly. I notice that the floor's not very clean. So I decide to give it a mop, but I can't get rid of the stains – in fact, the more I mop, the more there are, and I mop and mop but nothing happens. It starts to stress me out and I tell myself I'll never get it finished, and then one of the doors opens and it's my boss. He strides up to me, looking furious, walking all over the wet floor. I feel guilty and there's a sense of menace in the air. And then I realise I'm not wearing anything, I'm completely naked. He doesn't seem to notice this, he just keeps walking towards me as if there were nothing unusual about it, but it makes me feel really uncomfortable. That's when I wake up. I wonder what on earth it could mean.

Washing-up Liquid • deodorant • etc ... • Toothborush
Atonic accordian • 6 30 1804

Barbara

Estelle's got a chicory costume that she doesn't mind lending me. It's from some show she was in – 'Chicory chic'. There's a giant slice of ham that goes with it – that will be wrapped round the chicory and that's how we'll end it. With a followspot and the fireproof velvet curtains I've salvaged, it'll look fantastic. But before all that, I've got to finish my tax returns. It's so depressing.

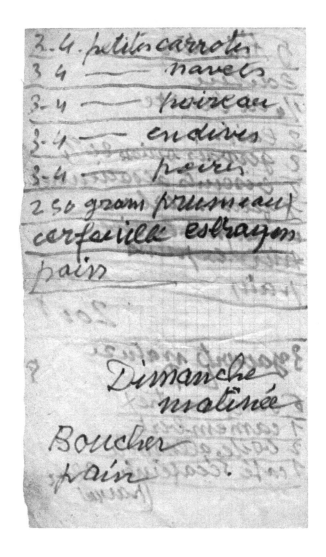

3–4 *little carrots* • 3 4 *turnips* • 3–4 *leeks* • 3–4 *endives*
3–4 *pears* • 250 *gram prunes* • *cherville tarragon* • *bread*
Sunday morning • *Butcher* • *bread*

Aliénor

We all have our doubts, our worries, all the time, that's normal. But praying is that time in the day when I press pause, when I switch off in all simplicity, in a heart-to-heart with Jesus. I tell the Lord that I love Him, I listen to Him through His Word, and I clear my head of all thoughts. The main thing is not to understand. Once you've understood that, the Holy Spirit is within us. I receive Jesus's love, and that gives me the strength to give love in return, everyday. Afterwards, I feel wonderful, I feel light – it's even better than going for a swim.

Christmass list • pork ham (from Paul) • gobstoppers
(large) • ~~BDC~~ *spirou comic subscription (* ~~6 years~~ *1 year or 6 month) • reel maron*
glacés • jokes and novelties • big trampoleen

Tobias

I don't understand the point of having a door in a water tower. There's no point – you can't open it because the inside is full of water. If you try and open it, for starters the water will create too much pressure, and even if you managed to open it by pushing really hard, all the water would come out all at once and you'd get soaked, or you could even drown. I suppose you could wear a diving suit. I saw the man who looks after the water tower, the other day, on the path – he was wearing grey trousers with pockets and carrying a toolbox. I didn't see him come out of the water tower … I missed that – he was leaving when I saw him. At any rate, he didn't look as if he'd got soaked. Maybe he's got some special way of creating a corridor in the middle of the water, so he can go in, like Moses parting the Red Sea in that film, with a false beard. Maybe there's a special super-strong magnet that repels the water. Afterwards, when he's come back out, he presses a button and the water resumes its normal form so nobody else can go inside. If it were up to me, I'd put a window in, rather than a door – then you could've used a ladder to get in from above. At the end of the day, I can't see why anybody would need to go inside a water tower – there's no point. I still wonder what it looks like, inside. Maybe there's secret stuff in there.

CLEAROUT

Franck

In today's world, I just want to say that – in terms of colleagues – there are many of us who find ourselves obliged to wait and see with regard to the years to come. The assignments we're on are clearly atypical – for those of us in our category, in order to progress, you have to remember that the main thing is that we're working under the auspices of the notion of self-motivation. The starting point – which is very simple – is that you can't ever let your proposed commitments be impacted by contingencies. Never. As I understand it, that's the most important thing. In other words, from a certain perspective, we're caught in a twin process extending from risk to opportunity. Everyone knows and everyone agrees that the issue at hand is complex and occasionally multifaceted from certain viewpoints, and at the same time – in my opinion – it will be increasingly so. That said, in terms of this question of the unknown, what it in fact brings into focus is the notion of any limitation that should implicitly be put in place, particularly at this time of decentralization.

fromage - crème fraiche - yaourts
2 Kg farine - 3 briques crème liquide
café -
2 beurre -

Bebert - 1 KO2R
1 Rouy

Sandrine - jambon blanc (5)
Steach hachés (6)
crème fraiche - gruyere rapé
2 pate brisée - Cousteron
café rouge - petites quenelles
assortiment fruits mer -

Marcelle - 1 Vire la vie
1 Kg sucre
1 torsette Riche
1 mocaroni Riche

---

*cheese • crème fraiche • yoghurts • 3 cartons single cream • 2 Kg
flour • coffee • 2 butter • <u>Bebert</u> • 1 KO2R • 1 Rouy • <u>Sandrine</u>
cooked ham (5) • minsed beef (6) • creme fraiche • grated gruyere
2 shortcrust pastry • cousteron • red coffee • small fish dumpling
seafood medley • <u>Marcelle</u> • 1 copy Fit Over Forty • 1 Kg sugar
1 Riche pasta twists • 1 Riche mocaroni*

Marcelle

In the latest *Fit Over Forty*, there's a really interesting article on sleep and how to activate your vital energy after the age of sixty by looking on the bright side of life. I cut it out to show it to Bébert. What you have to do is eat well, identify the source of your vitality, and the main thing they emphasise is the need to remain really active. I never have time to be bored, which is exactly what I was saying to Sandrine only yesterday – she didn't believe me, but I'm busier now than when I was working. Look, I said to her, on Mondays I've got pottery, on Tuesday afternoons I go to the stadium with the old people's home. This week, it was my turn to take cake for everyone, so I spent the morning making my apple Swiss roll with almond flour, using the recipe my mother gave me. I got started on it early because it's not as nice when it's warm, and it needed time to cool down. Otherwise I could have done it the day before and wrapped it in clingfilm, but I've run out of that – I'll have to remember to add that to the list. Often on Wednesdays, I have the grandkids to keep me busy, and every fortnight I go to my painting evening class – I've only missed the Wednesday during the Easter holidays, and that was because of the coach trip to Chauvet Cave and we slept over. On Fridays, me and Monique go to aquagym – well, we do when the trains are running. You never know what to expect with the SNCF. 'Slack, Neglectful, Careless, and Feckless' is what my son-in-law calls them. The other day, instead of the train there was a coach service, because of some heatwave alert, so the heat bends the track out of shape – I ask you, with the weather being stormy half the time. And of course, it would never have occurred to them to warn us the train had been cancelled – we only found out when we'd got to the platform at Laroche-Migennes, and then it was too late, we were stuck. Two hours it took us to get home. When Marine is in charge, at least, the trains will run on time.

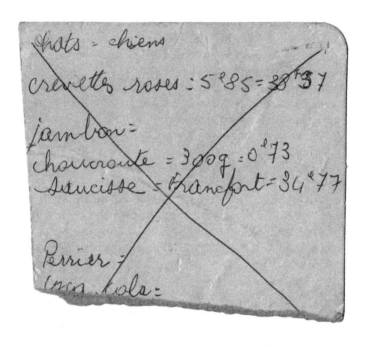

*cats = dogs • pink shrimp = 5ᶜ85 = 33ᶜ57 • ham =
sauerkraut 300 g = 0ᶜ73 • sausage = Franfurter = 34ᶜ77
Perrier = • coca cola =*

Édith

'Be thee good, O my Grief, and sit thyself more still' – who's that by again? It must be Baudelaire or Mallarmé – one of those Symbolists, anyway. 'The evening you'd called for and blabla here it is, fer-some-its-gift-is-peace, fer-others-just-worries ...'. It's awful losing your memory like this. The worst time was when we visited the cemetery at Charleville. I'd wanted to gather my thoughts at Rimbaud's tomb – not because I like him particularly, but anyway. I recited the odd verse of his by way of homage: 'Above the rooftops, shines the sky, so blue, so calm!' It was only when I was back home, that evening, that I realised I'd quoted Verlaine, that I'd mixed up my poets.

Lacet, pain, pile, museau,

Laces, bread, battery, brawn,

Enzo

If you want a kilo of feathers compared to a kilo of lead, you need at least ten kilos. Or else you have to wet them.

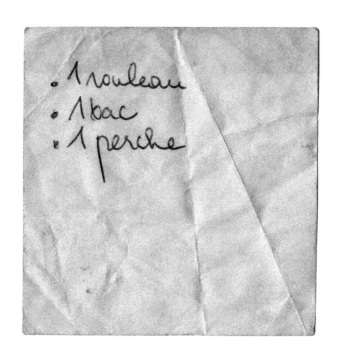

1 roller • 1 tray • 1 pole

Audrey

I'm going to have to find a diving club for oldies, because the last time I went to Aquaforum it was full of legionnaires in war-machine mode. The instructor looked like a baddie from a James Bond film, and I was the only woman there. I go there for fun – not to learn how to sink the *Rainbow Warrior*.

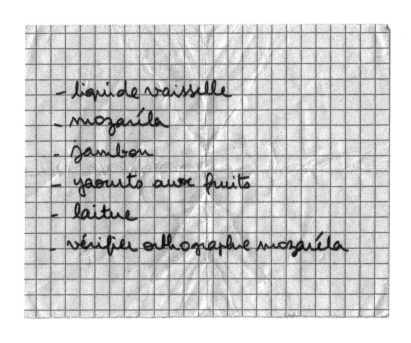

- liquide vaisselle
- mozaréla
- jambon
- yaourts aux fruits
- laitue
- vérifier orthographe mozaréla

washing-up liquid • mozarela • ham • fruit yoghurts
lettuce • check spelling of mozarela

James

I'll be glad when I have my appointment with the doctor, later, so he can confirm my suspicions about having cancer, which I've discovered thanks to the Internet. That way, I shan't have been worrying over nothing.

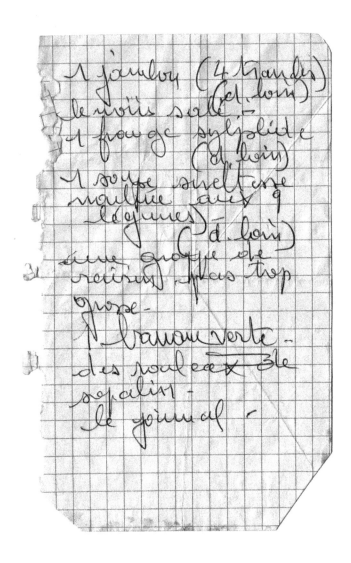

1 ham (4 slices) (f far) the least salted • sylphide cheese
(f far) • 1 sveltesse 9 vegetable instant soup (f far)
one bunch of grapes not too big • 1 <u>green</u> banana
1 kitchen roll • the newspaper

Émilie

To begin with, I had to see a doctor, owing to this cooling-off period palaver. Nowadays, I think they've stopped that. He looked at me, like a schoolteacher, and told me to think it through, that women had lost sight of their primary vocation, namely procreation or perpetuating the species. That today it was unfortunate, but all people thought about was their own personal interests. That blended families worked really well, these days. And that at my age, by the time I'd found someone and established the relationship enough to be in a position to want to have a child, it would be too late, and that that would make me awfully bitter. That this was my last chance. I half-expected him to say, 'With your ugly mug, no one will want you'. I said nothing. I just needed him to sign the piece of paper.

- Alcool à brûler
- mouchoirs en papier
- schampoing
- savon pour la barbe
- lames
- regarder amaciador. marque Corinne de Farme.
- 1 savon.

Methylated spirit • paper tissues • schampoo • soap for beard • blades • look for Corinne de Farme brand amaciador • 1 soap

Florian

I'm 24 years old, I'm young, and I don't mind treating myself, every now and again. I'm someone who likes to party, and I like making the most of things. It doesn't have to get messy, y'know, just make the most of life, of every moment, every second. So I enjoy it to the max – I'd rather spend my money on that than spend it on drugs or whatever. We all have our little indulgences, and my little indulgences are cars and clothes. A white Porsche convertible is a babe-magnet – let's not pretend otherwise. You get more girls with one of those. And it's not so hard to get a beautiful car like that – you just need some ambition in life, and you need to work. I pretty much work a seven-day week, you see. There's no secret. Apart from that, I have the benefit of still living with my parents, so every now and again I treat myself, y'know.

GARLIC POWDER · GROUND PEPPER · SALT · OIL · THYME · ONIONS
SAUSAGE WITH LENTILS · CASSOULET · TUNA · RICE · PASTA
POTATOES · CARROT · COURGETTES · BROCOLI · SALAD · TOMATOES
CUCUMBER · LEMON · EGGS · YOGHURTS · GERVAIS
BUTTER · HAM · ROSETTE/SALAMI · HOT-DOGS · CHICKEN BREAST
PIZZA · MEAT · CHIPS · GRATTED CHEESE · FRUIT · SPONGE
SCRAPER · DISHCLOTH · CLEANING WIPES

Margaux

I feel like there's something I've forgotten. I shouldn't've drunk any coffee – every time I drink coffee, I feel like there's something I've forgotten. What on earth could I have forgotten? I can't see. It's the filter coffee – turns out it contains more caffeine than the percolated stuff they serve in bars, but you wouldn't think so. You'd think it were weaker because it contains more water, but no – in fact it contains *more* caffeine. I hear it prevents some people from getting to sleep – turns out the effects last up to six hours later. I don't know about that, but for me it does something to my brain so I sort of get this feeling that I've forgotten to switch the light off or turn the oven off or something else, but what?

~~QUID HAND SOAP~~ · ~~PRE-COOKED BREAD~~ · ~~LION CHOCOLATE~~ · ~~TEA~~ · ~~NUTELLA~~
~~MILK~~ · CAKES · ~~COOK/APERITIF~~ · B'FAST DOUDOU · ~~JUICE~~ · ~~DRINKS?~~
~~COMPOTES~~ · ~~TOILET PAPER~~ · ~~CADUM SHOWER GEL~~ · ~~TAMPONS~~
~~OLL-ON DEOD~~ · ~~// DOUDOU~~ · SAFORELLE · ~~LIYA SHOWER GEL~~ · ~~BODY CREAM~~
~~TISSUES~~ · ~~COTTON BUDS STICK~~ · ~~FACIAL CLEANSER~~
~~BABY WIPES~~ · ~~MAXI BABY PADS~~ · ~~BUDGET NAPPIES~~
DEXERYL · ~~KETCHUP~~ · ~~LIYA WATER~~ · ~~VEGETABLE PEELER~~

2 butter

Lou-Anne

In all honesty, by general consent, it's in bed that I really shine. But I can't tell anyone that. People can say, 'So-and-so is an excellent cook – you should try her *blanquette de veau*'. But try saying, 'So-and-so is a great fuck – you should try her blowjob'. You can't. So everyone thinks I'm useless.

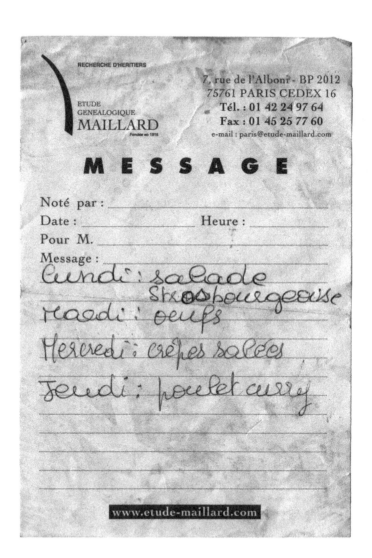

RECHERCHE D'HERITIERS

ETUDE
GENEALOGIQUE
MAILLARD
Fondée en 1916

7, rue de l'Alboni - BP 2012
75761 PARIS CEDEX 16
Tél. : 01 42 24 97 64
Fax : 01 45 25 77 60
e-mail : paris@etude-maillard.com

MESSAGE

Noté par : _____
Date : _____ Heure : _____
Pour M. _____
Message : _____

Lundi : salade Strasbourgeoise
Mardi : oeufs
Mercredi : crêpes salées
Jeudi : poulet curry

www.etude-maillard.com

Monday: Strasbourg salad • Tuesday: eggs
Wednesday: savoury pancakes • Thursday: chicken curry

Jean-Pierre

When I asked for a translation of the hundredth abbreviation that had flown straight over my head, some little joker took it upon himself to explain – with all the smugness bestowed on the young – what BNF stood for. 'It's the Bibliothèque Nationale de France, Jean-Pierre'. It's become an obsession, and it just complicates everything by turning 'work breakdown structure' into WBS, or by saying MEDEF, ONU, RTT, CDD ... It's baffling, and it's not even French. Yesterday, I was reading that – according to the *Guinness Book of Records* – the longest acronym in the world is Russian. Fifty-four characters it has. From what I understood, it was for some factory specialising in concrete. When you reach that level, you've gone beyond the realms of administrative madness and entered the purely abstract.

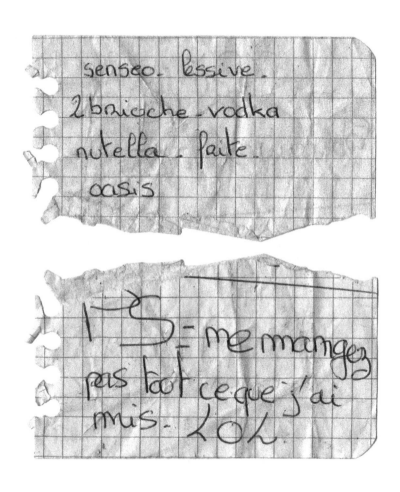

senseo • washing • 2 brioche • vodka • nutella • chips • oasis
PS = don't eat everything I've put. LOL

Jade

Keep your eyes off the new neighbour – I've got first dibs on *him*. I'll fess, when I saw him on the landing, I didn't know who it was – I only realized later that it was him who'd just moved into 6B. I swear, the guy's totally hot. Brown hair, brown eyes. He seems nice too. Not sure how old he is, but I'd say about 26. Maybe he's a model, or he works in fashion or in a clothes shop. He's seriously got style. When I bumped into him, he was wearing a grey V-neck tee, with some American writing on it, and it was obvious that underneath he was hench. Like the guy in the perfume ad, where he like dives in the water in slo-mo, super-fit, with abs like speed bumps and everything. I hope he didn't see me though, cos when I bumped into him, my hair was literally like Guantanamo, cos my straightener had just died on me. More made in China shit – that's what you get if you don't buy the real thing. Embarrassing or what? I hope he's not got a girlfriend. Looking at him, you'd swear he's got some American name, like 'Tyler' or 'Kyle', but actually I saw on his letterbox that he's called Frédéric Lassagne – okay, not so classy but who cares, it suits him anyway. I've got to get his mobile number somehow, y'know, to tell him, I dunno, maybe say, 'Hi, have you just moved in? Jade here. I share 6D with a mate, if you wanna drop by'. No, that sucks. I must call Naima and ask her advice – she'll be well jel. All *her* neighbours are repulsive. I'm telling you, *that* girl's been cursed.

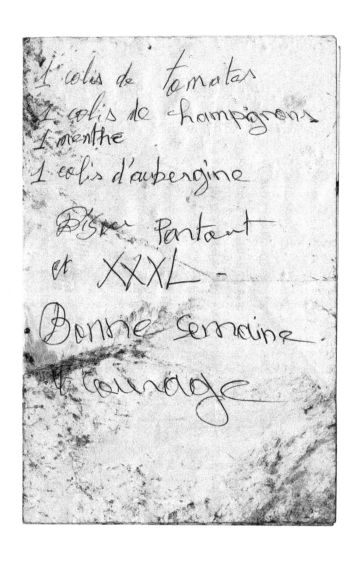

1 tomato puray • 1 mushroom puray • 1 aubergine puray
Kiss you All over and XXXL • Have a good week and Good Luck

Sofian

The worst job I've ever had was working as a museum attendant. Eight hours, every day, sat next to a video of a barking dog. At night, it haunted my dreams. Then I was a waiter, which wasn't bad, thanks to the tips especially, but the boss was a wanker, and I left. Then I did my back in, working for a removals firm. It's not that I'm lazy – I just ain't got the build for that sort of thing. But the best of all was when I worked for the hospital, as a courier transporting organs for transplants. I was getting paid for what I enjoy most in life: driving fast. And it was legal. 'Blue light driving' they call it. I'd turn up somewhere, get the load, stick the flashing light on the roof, and – hold tight, darlin' – put the pedal to the metal.

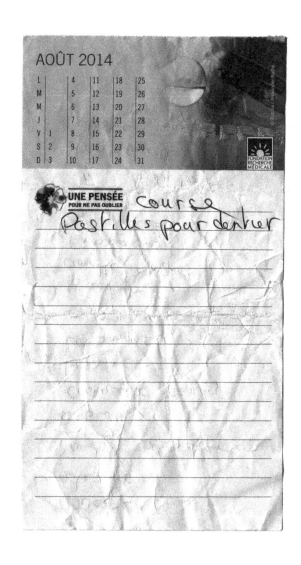

AOÛT 2014

L		4	11	18	25
M		5	12	19	26
M		6	13	20	27
J		7	14	21	28
V	1	8	15	22	29
S	2	9	16	23	30
D	3	10	17	24	31

FONDATION
RECHERCHE
MÉDICALE

UNE PENSÉE
POUR NE PAS OUBLIER

course
Pastilles pour dentier

shopping • Denture cleaning tablets

Liliane

With everything you read about, these days, there's certainly reason to worry about things. For some time now I've been getting the magazine *True Crime*. My husband reckons it's a load of old nonsense, that everything in it is made up, and I'm developing morbid obsessions. I, on the other hand, don't think that keeping up with what's happening in the real world means I'm developing morbid obsessions. In life, not everything's a bed of roses. Whatever, nowadays I always ask the fuel attendant to fill my car up – I'm too frightened of being burned alive.

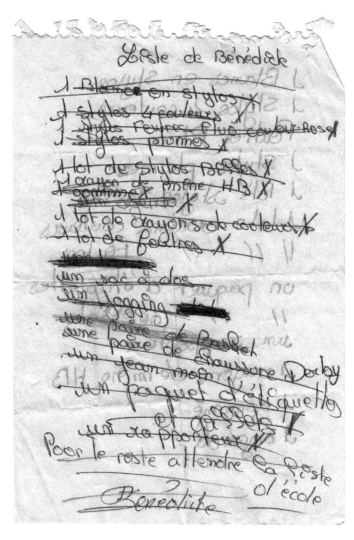

Bénédicte's list • 1 White in pens • 1 4-colour pen
1 Pink colour Fluorescent Felt-tip pen • 1 fountain pen • 1 pack of pens
Ballpoint • 1 lead pencil HB • 1 eraser • 1 diary • 1 pack of
colouring pencils • 1 pack of felt tips • a pencil case • a rucksack
an adidas tracksuit • a pair of Trainers • a pair of Derby shoes
a packet of stickers and paper hole reinforcers • a protractor
For the rest wait for the list from school • Bénédicte

Bénédicte

I wonder who I'll be with and which form tutor we'll get – I hope it's miss Toébat cos she takes Year 9. And I can't wait to see the girls again. Except for Angèle – I won't talk to *her* ever again, not even in a dream. She spat in my shampoo and cut my favourite knickers into strips, the bitch. I really hope I'll be in the same class as Maxime, but he's taken Spanish as a second language. Anyway, Coline told me that Annabelle had told her that he'd split up with Nawelle over the summer, meaning he's single. What clothes am I going to wear? I really have to ask mum to take me shopping for some new clothes, but she'll almost certainly say no, cos she's already got me a new bag. It's so, so stylish, I'm so happy – it's the same as the one Jessica got for her birthday. I'll wait 'til Monday evening. When she gets back from work, she's tired and hasn't got the energy to say no to me. I'll beg and say it can count as an early Christmas present, or I'll be happy to pay her the money back in instalments, using my pocket money or the cash gran will surely give me for my name day. I'd just never live it down if I went back to school wearing the same jeans as last year, cos the fashion's totally changed and now the must-have is boyfriend jeans, except that's fake cos I don't have a boyfriend, unless Maxime wants to go out with me, but that's not going to happen before we get back to school, so I need it before then, so that's it.

gel express Apta tube
gaut caoutchouc 6 1/2.
        (résistant)
coloration M. Baïkal
Blond très très clair cendré doré
Coloration eugène color.
Blond très très clair naturel
crème en Pot nutri extrême
Jacques Dessange Pot Jaune
crème en Pot pour le corps.

tube Apta <u>express laundry gel</u> • <u>rubber glove</u> 6 ½ (resistant)
<u>M Baikal hair dye</u> Very very light ashy golden blonde
<u>eugène color hair dye</u> Very very light natural blonde
<u>nutri extreme cream in Pot</u> Jacques Dessange Yellow Pot
<u>cream in Pot</u> for body

Laurence

Fifteen years I've been telling him that tumblers go on the LEFT side of the glass cupboard and stemmed glasses go on the RIGHT. Fifteen years, and he still can't get that into his head. Men have no sense of the practical whatsoever – it must be in their genes. It makes me think that if I weren't here to think of everything, then nothing would ever get done. Just yesterday, I saved his wallet and everything in it, yet again – right at the last second – from a 60°C cotton cycle. He'd forgotten to take it out of the back pocket. And it's not for want of telling him, over and over again, to be careful. It drives me crazy. Next time, I'll leave it in there, and the only person he'll have to blame is himself.

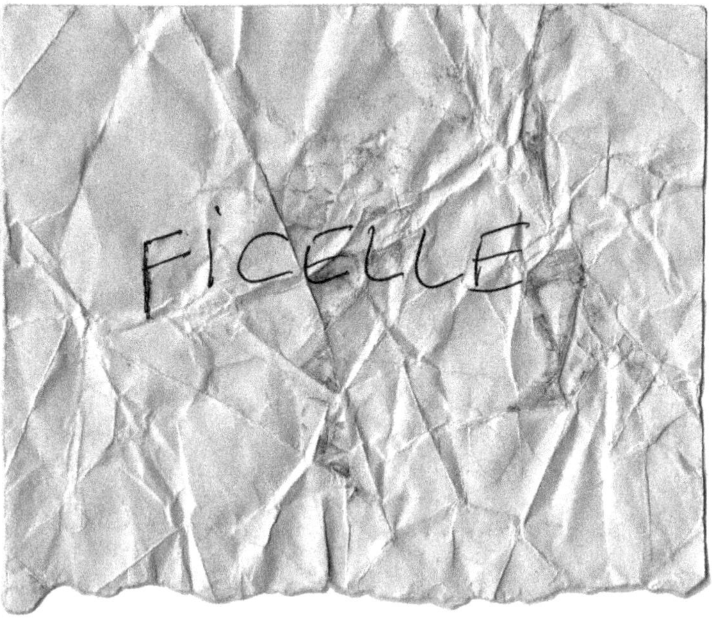

STRING

Théo

I always make a big deal about it, but when you get started, in two hours it's done and dusted. This time, it'd been a good three years since I'd sorted anything. All my bills and letters were stuffed into the drawer of the cupboard in the hall. There must've been about fifteen envelopes that hadn't even been opened. When I went through them, I discovered that *Gaz Service* had been writing to me regularly over the last few years, sending me reminders, follow-up letters, cancellations, and a load of missed appointments with phantom gas men. It also turns out that – two years ago – they'd sent someone to come and change the meter. I didn't have a clue about any of this, what with not opening my mail. It's like discovering that – for all that time – a parallel universe existed next to mine, but I wasn't aware of it at all.

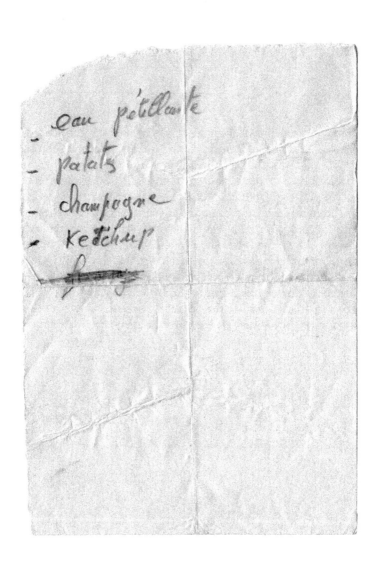

eau pétillante

- _patats_
- _champagne_
- _ketchup_

sparkling water • spuds • champagne • ketchup • cheese

Alicia

It turns out George Michael has been to Switzerland for treatment, and it cost 70,000 euros a week. What I'd like to know is what services they provide to justify such a price tag. Maybe they replace your blood entirely, like they did for Keith Richards. Or perhaps they make your bed, three times a day, with sheets of wild silk, or they have species on the verge of extinction on the menu, like 'pulled panda' or 'leg of white rhino', and you can have a bath in vintage champagne. It's like stars and their weird rider lists. Madonna's rider insists on a brand-new toilet seat in every new venue. Jennifer Lopez will only stay in hotel rooms that are filled with white lilies. For Lady Gaga, it has to be odourless cheese served on a bed of ice. Then there's Mariah Carey, who – I kid you not – has an assistant whose job it is to collect her used chewing gum. But the best of the lot is what Britney Spears asks for ... In her dressing room, the M&Ms she's served have to be red. That means they have to pay a guy just to sort through packets and packets of M&Ms – it's downright smart. I wonder what I'd have as a rider, if I were a star. You have to admit, it takes some imagination.

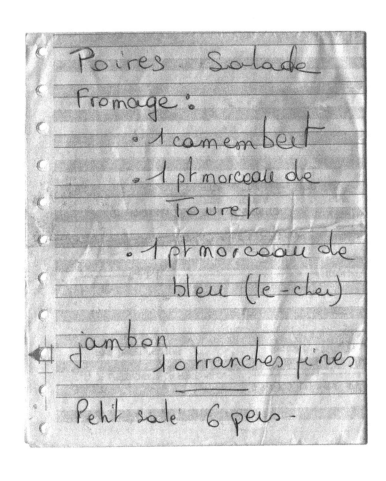

Poires   Salade

Fromage:

• 1 camembert

• 1 pt morceau de
Touret

• 1 pt morceau de
bleu (le -cher)

jambon
10 tranches fines

Petit salé 6 pers -

*Pears • Salad • Cheese: 1 camembert, 1 little bit of Touret, 1 little
bit of blue (expensive one) • ham 10 thin slices
Salt pork 6 ppl*

Marie-Hélène

Obviously, all her father and I want is for her to be happy, but we don't understand her. When we were her age, what we wanted was a good job, a house, and modern comforts. We worked jolly hard to pay for all that. With her qualifications, she could have got a job anywhere she liked. But no. She and her boyfriend decided to leave the Paris region to set up home in the darkest depths of the Ardèche. The very idea. It's true, the scenery is beautiful. But it's very remote, and you should see the conditions they live in. They haven't even got a loo! Instead, there's a bucket you throw sawdust into, and then you have to empty it. It's not normal. She's also got it into her head to wash her laundry by hand using wood ash. Even in my grandmother's time, people hadn't done that in ages. Back then, they were over the moon when washing machines came out. And using ash can't get the laundry clean, in my opinion. But she won't listen to a word I say, she's always been stubborn, she digs her heels in. Consequently, they stink like billy goats. The last straw was when they wanted us to sleep in a log cabin, with no electricity. Enough's enough! So I ended up saying something. In the end, we still stayed with them for two days, but the atmosphere was tense. I really hope this hippie nonsense is just a phase she's going through. It worries me ... Fortunately, her sister's far more sensible. She's given us two beautiful grandchildren.

coarse salt • peas

Amélie

Because of the girls from the Crazy Horse Cabaret that we'd watch on the telly on New Year's Eve – pretty much identical, perfect, and hand-picked – I used to think all women's breasts were the same, and that when I grew up, I'd have breasts exactly like theirs. If I'd known I was going to end up with these two watermelons, I'd have made the most of it and slept on my stomach while I still could.

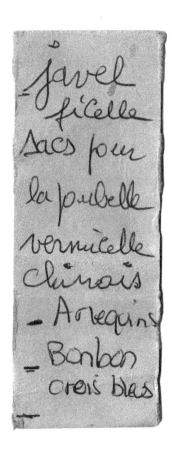

*bleach • string • bags for the dustbin • vermicelli • Chinese
Arlequin sweets • Crois bleu sweets*

Olivier

Solzhenitsyn describes it very well in *One Day in the Life of Ivan Denisovich*. A system based on chance, oppression at the hands of the guards, the back-breaking work, the bone-numbing cold, the interminable waiting for disgusting food, and the brutal law that means only the strongest get through it. Honestly, no – in every single respect, I do not miss boarding school. There's not an animal on this earth that would have survived what I went through.

2 WINE • 1 milk • ~~wite~~ onyons • 1 milk
2 WINE • 4 RUM • 1 milk • ~~grapes~~ cherries
1 milk • 3 WINE • 1 camembert • 1 milk • 1 bread

Albert

For a long time, I'd go to bed early. But now I'm retired, it's fine – I can carry on watching films into the late-evening slot.

Anti hair loss Lotion

Gilles

For the time being, it's still okay – it's thinning a bit at the top of my forehead, but if I don't lower my head, nobody will notice. I could always dye it – people do that, these days. It would make me look younger. The annoying thing with that is that people would know. Even when you're talking about guys who can afford a really good hairdresser. Look at Paul McCartney, for example, or François Hollande – you can tell it's way too dark. They look like they've dyed their hair themselves with RégéColor, at home, in their bathroom sink. Now, Johnny Hallyday … he's something else. He has these crazy highlights, but you can only get away with that if you're in showbiz. If you're not, you look like a clown. But even if you take a more discreet approach, it doesn't look natural. There's always the solution of shaving it all off. But when I run my hand over my head, it feels bumpy, and I don't think it would look so great. Another thing I could do is grow a beard … to divert attention. That would give me a certain look. I have tried that already, but – after a while – it itches, and my wife finds it spiky and says I look scruffy. Even a moustache is out, as far as she's concerned. I tell you – in life, you really can't always get what you want.

Beer • milk • Cough mixture • crème fraiche • Tinned mackerel

René

It cost me 72 euros, which is expensive. In old money, that would be about 50,000 francs. Or 500 new francs. I still get confused. For example, I can remember that the grey packet with the red stripe I used to buy for my pipe cost 80 centimes, and then it went up to 1 franc. Nowadays, a packet of tobacco costs 5 euros, at least, which is 40 francs, or 40,000 old francs. These days, I couldn't afford to smoke. Not unless I played the Lottery.

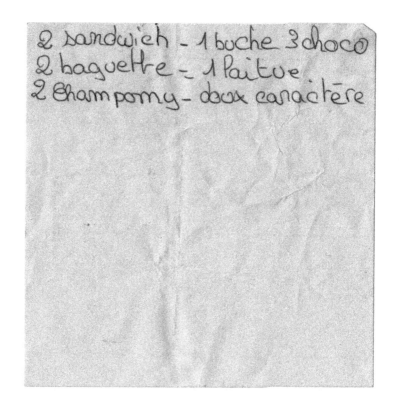

2 sandwich - 1 buche 3 choco
2 baguette = 1 laitue
2 Champomy - doux caractère

*2 sandwiches • 1 Yule log 3 choco • 2 baguettes • 1 lettuce
2 Champomy • soft character*

Lilou

When I discovered 1D, the one I fancied in the group was Niall. I wrote a story where it's all made-up, all about him. It's about a girl called Lyloo, who's 23 and she's been working in London for three years as a model. She's 5'7", has blue-green almond-shaped eyes and silky black hair. She's on a photo shoot for swimming costumes, and she meets five guys having their own photo shoot before her. She thinks they're all really cute, they introduce themselves, and they decide to go for a drink. Louis has an Orangina, Harry has a coffee, Niall has a Pepsi, Zayn has an apple juice, Liam has a white coffee, and Lyloo has lemonade with mint. She finds out that Niall is single and that it's been three months since he broke up with his girlfriend who's a dancer. The next day, they see each other again and they're really, really happy. They jump into each other's arms, and Lyloo makes up her mind to say something to Niall. She says, 'Y'know, Niall, since yesterday, I can't stop thinking about you'. And he says, 'Same here – I can't stop thinking about you. I think it was love at first sight'. Then they catch up with the others and grab a burger and some pasta. A few days later, cos they're still together and everything's going well, Lyloo decides to move in with the guys. A month later, everything's still going really well.

TP Fire • *1 milk* • *WINE* • *WALAIT* • *CAT* • *MEAt* • *COFFee*
CHOCO • *coat Hair Balls* • *ONe spud* • *ACTIVIANNATO*

Mickaël

It was useless trying to move away from her – Josiane from accounts was right in my face, talking at me, and she kept moving forward, like a steamroller, until I ended up trapped, with my back against the photocopier, like a cornered animal, unable to move, unable to do anything. In a previous life, I bet she must've been an interrogator. Either that or it's cos she wants my body.

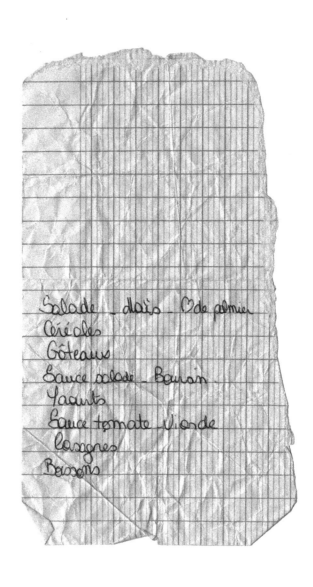

Salade _ maïs _ ♡ de palmier
Céréales
Gâteaux
Sauce salade _ Boursin
Yaourts
Sauce tomate viande
lasagnes
Boissons

Salad • Sweetcorn • <3 of palm • Cereals • Cakes • Salad dressing
Boursin • Yoghurts • Tomato sauce • Meat • lasagna • Drinks

Coralie

On Saturday, for the party, I wore my black dress – *THE* dress, with the *décolletage* ... Maybe it was a bit *ooh la la*. But the good thing about it is that guys don't really focus on the conversation, so you don't have to come out with any intelligent stuff. Even so, it soon gets boring. And then there's the other girls, who tend to start scowling. On the other hand, it's the best when I have a *problemo* with the car. Last time, the guy at the garage simply refused to take my money. I think I'll wear it again next week, when the plumber comes round for the boiler. With a bit of luck, he'll knock something off the price.

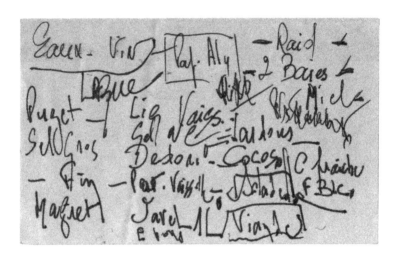

Water • WINE • lacquer • Puget • Salt Coarse • End • Duck Breast Fillet • Kitch foil
Wash Liq • Toilet gel • Dedori • Ptoes Wash • Bleach. 1 L • S pong • Trek
2 Berries • Honey • Oli • Crapontelly • lardons • Cocos • C fraiche
F BLC • salad • Meat

Cyrille

I've had the results back from my blood test but I can't understand a word of it. Next to my total cholesterol, there's 5.32 mmol but it should be less than 5.18, and 2.09 gl which should be less than 2.00, and then there's HDL, that's at 1.23 mmol but it should be above 1.55, and 0.49 gl, which should be above 0.60, and for LDL it's 3.61 mmol and 1.40 gl, but it doesn't say what it should be, so I don't know if it's serious or not.

1 kg viande porc
4 saucisses
4 boudins aux oignons

sucre   poudre amande
120 gr noix   chocolat
coca zero

12 oeufs
800 gr mascarpone
biscuits cuillère
extrait café + 1 saucisson

1 kg meat pork • 4 sausages • 4 black puddings with onions • sugar
120 gr of nuts • cola zero • 12 eggs • powdered almonds • chocolate
800 gr of mascarpone • sponge fingers • coffee extract + salami

Mallaury

By tomorrow, I've got to get rid of every last bit of tiramisu. It's nothing but fat and sugar, but after that, I'm giving it up. Anyway, nobody starts a diet on a Saturday. I've skim-read a fair few articles about that super-high-protein diet that celebs are on, and it sounds great. Lose ten kilos in a month, they say, without any effort. You don't have to deprive yourself of anything, and you don't feel hungry because you can eat as much as you like, when you like, provided it's meat or fish. Apparently, if you fancy getting out of bed in the middle of the night to eat three steaks, you can – you just can't have any chips. What's more, you're not allowed to eat salad or vegetables, which suits me fine cos I'm not mad about either, generally. Nah, it'll be a walk in the park – not least cos I don't mind having ham or black pudding for breakfast. Quite the opposite. It's funny, cos I'd never have believed you could lose weight by eating sausages – it just goes to show how sometimes you believe stuff that's not true.

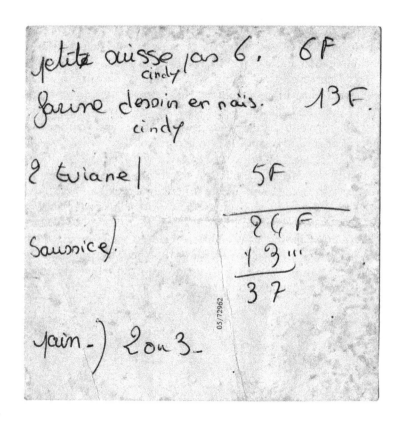

Petite suisse by 6. Cindy 6 F • corn flour desert cindy 13 F
2 Eviane 5 F • Sausage • bread 2 or 3 • 27 F 13 ... / 37

Magali

What I'd like to know is if – at the end of the 24 months of the moratorium – the Banque de France will carry on administering our accounts, and if it will still show on our credit rating. It's like having a criminal record – it doesn't exactly cover us in glory, and yet we're good, honest people. We always paid on time – ask any loan company and they couldn't deny it. The problem is that there'll be seven different consumer credit bills to pay back at the same time, and that could take us years. To begin with, it was free. And then there were charges, and we didn't understand what was happening to us. If I'd known we were both going to end up unemployed, I would never have bought the calfskin leather sofa. To cap it all, it's too big for the living room, and it's a bit stiff to sit on.

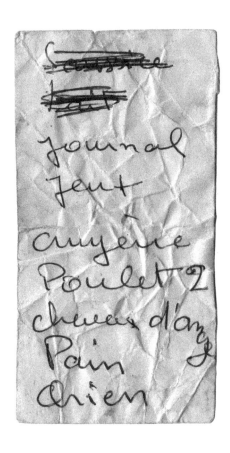

Sausage • *Milk* • Newspaper • Crossword mag • Gruyère • Chicken 2
angel hair • Bread • dog

Michel

Dad doesn't recognise me any more. Well … to be precise, he doesn't recognise anyone anymore. It's funny how you keep hoping, despite everything. The other day, I got all excited – turns out it was over nothing. For a second, I thought he was in remission, that he was starting to remember his mother tongue, and that – maybe – he'd recognised me. But the nurse said there was no reason to get too excited … If he was saying, 'Kinder! Kinder!' when he saw me, it was because of the Kinder Buenos I bring him every time I come to see him.

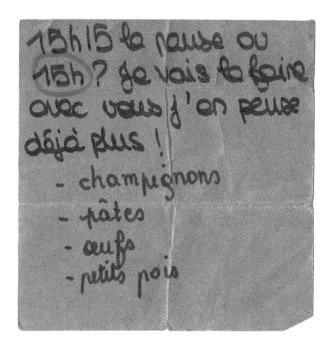

Break at 3:15 pm or 3 pm? I'm going to do it with you I just can't bear it any more! • mushrooms • pasta • eggs • peas

Alison

I'm so fucking bored. In an ideal world, Ryan Gosling would turn up on his white horse, he'd whisk me off to a five-star hotel, cover me in ambrosia, and we'd drink nectar together.

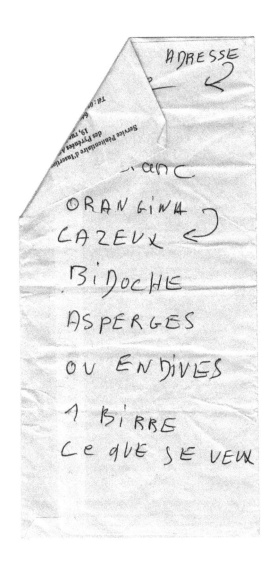

*ADDRESS • FIZY ORANGINA • MEAT • ASPARAGUS OR
ENDIVES • 1 BEEER WhateVER I WANT*

Kyllian

The title'll be "'Sgonna kick off, 'sgonna kick off'. It'll be fuckin'
massive.
  Yo brah huh huh
  One two one two
  Brah you don't wanna piss me off
  'Snot a good time 'sgonna kick off
  I'm not in the mood
  Diss me you're screwed
  You're a loser brah
  You think I care
  A loser like
  Riding a bike
  I'm king of the dark
  In the car park
  Anvil's the name
  Bang what a shame
It's not finished yet. I don't know what comes next – we'll see. You
gotta find inspiration from your own personal experience. You gotta
work at the style, it's a craft – it don't just write itself. Gonna have
to find a beat to go with the flow. Then it's showtime. You gotta
go for what you know. Big time.

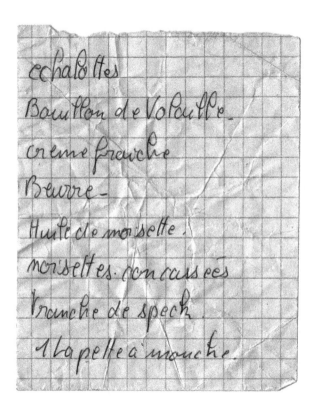

echalottes
Bouillon de Volaille_
creme fraiche
Beurre_
Huile de noisette.
noisettes. concassées
tranche de speck
1 La pelle à mouche

shalotts • Chicken Stock • creme fraiche • Butter • Azelnut
oil • crushed hazelnuts • sliced speck • 1 fly swatter

Claude

When one is polite, one says that it's a wine that should be laid down. But I said it was bloody revolting. Because it's true.

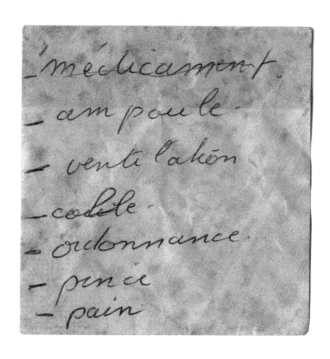

- médicament.
- ampoule.
- ventilation
- colle.
- ordonnance.
- pince
- pain

tablets • capsules • ventilation • glue • prescription • tweezers • bread

Madeleine

Well, they're saying it's going to snow. Winter's set in, at last. At home, when you're sat by the fire, you don't realise a thing. But in the kitchen, it says it's 8 degrees. To be fair, that is a bit chilly. But really, we're not going to all the bother of having the heating done again – not at our age. It's too late. We should have had a better heating system fitted when we bought the house, and back then, nobody did that. All you have to do is put an extra jumper or two on – and they say it's better for your health if your head's in cool, fresh air when you sleep. Anyway, in the old days, it was a lot worse – in the house I grew up in, only the kitchen was heated, and we never complained. That's just how it was. Of an evening, my father would put one briquette in the range, and that was your lot. Mind, we were in Lorraine, and you can't say the climate there's particularly clement. Of course, these days, it's not the same. Kids today need comfort. If they've not got a microwave, it's the end of the world. And they think it's normal to be wearing short sleeves, inside, even in winter. They're not used to it. Things were different when we were brought up. Back then, we didn't think things could be any other way. And I'll tell you this: I was cold throughout my entire childhood.

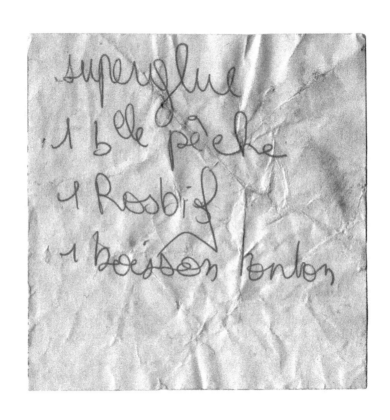

superglue • 1 btl peach • 1 Roast beef • 1 tonton drink

Sabine

Being happy is just a question of wanting to be happy. People ask me what my secret is. I don't know what to say really, I just made a choice to be positive, simple as that. In my opinion, you always have to look on the bright side of life, see the glass as half full, and when things aren't going so well, just laugh. When you laugh, you look good, and it really winds up the idiots. I'm not saying everything that's happened to me has been good – far from it. I've had my fair share of disasters, just like everyone else. Life's a shit sandwich, yeah, but if you leave it at that, you end up just giving up. You might as well curl up and wait to die. So what I prefer to tell myself is that I can't smell a thing and the sandwich on my plate has lovely Nutella in it.

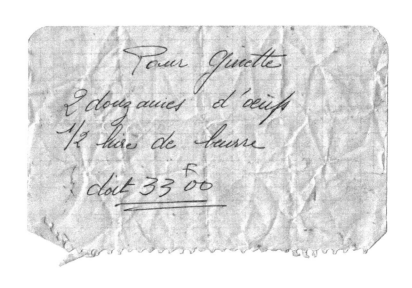

For Ginette • 2 dozen eggs • ½ pounds of butter • <u>owes 33 F 00</u>

Thérèse

Seriously!? Who the hell does Ginette think she is? Last Sunday, at the market, she asked if I could loan her the money for her shopping, because apparently she didn't have any change. And if you think she'd have paid me back, fat chance. What a leech. Come to think of it, the other day, I kissed her on both cheeks when I ran into her ... I'd have been better off kissing her dog's arse.

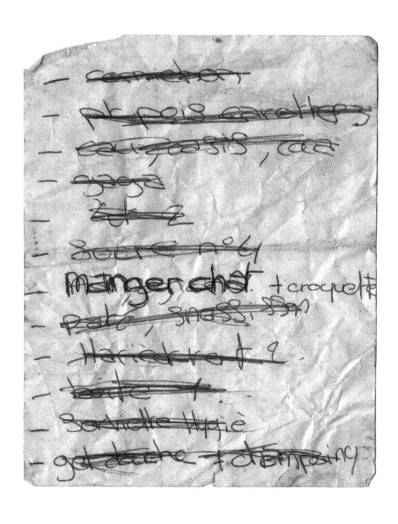

gherkins • peas carrots 3 • water, oasis, cola • gaga • zut 2
sugar no 4 • cat food + kibble • paté, saussages • Green beans 2
tin 1 • sanit towels • shower gel + schampoo

Jade

My life is fucked. I feel like a total loser. No one will ever want to go out with me ever again. I'll end up on my own, like that woman they found after it had been a week and she'd been eaten by her Labrador. What's going to happen to me, now he's gone? I feel so, so sad – I can't stop crying. He was the one. We were supposed to get married, he was supposed to be the father of my kids, and we were supposed to grow old together, that's what was planned. Not for him to go and stay at his cousin's on holiday, and then dump me by text, just two weeks before the start of the school year. I'm so, so unhappy – I miss him like crazy. I'll never fall in love with anyone else ever again. Impossible. I'll love only him, for the rest of my life, and I'll end up left on the shelf. But in my case, if there were no more food for him, I don't think my cat could ever eat me. As it is, he already gets grumpy when he's not given the right brand.

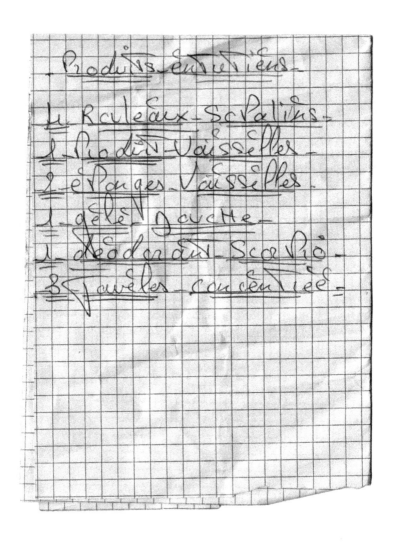

Produits entretiens

4 Rouleaux Sopalins
1 Produit Vaisselle
2 éPonges Vaisselle
1 gelé Douche
1 déodorant ScoRio
8 Javelet concentrée

Cleaning products • 4 Big KiTchen Rolls • 1 Washing Up Liquid
2 sPonge Scourers • 1 Shower jell • 1 ScoRPio deodorant
3 Bottles consentrated Bleach

Mickaël

That slag reported me to the police. Seeing as she's such an ugly cow, she should be bloody well flattered someone took an interest in her. When you go round turning men on, showing your arse off in tight-fitting mini-shorts, you can't come crying later, saying you had no idea. These woke feminist bitches are all lezzers – all they need is a good seeing-to. Some real cock, that's what they need. But I'll leave that job to someone else. My dick might not be able to see anything, but I've got my standards.

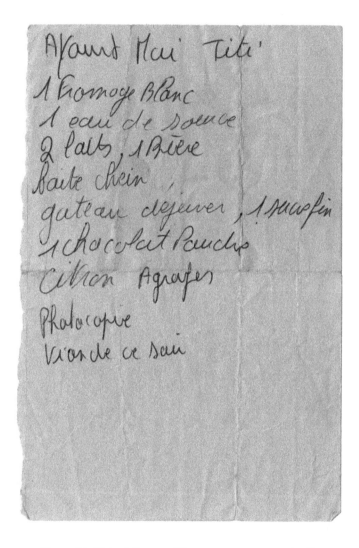

Yogurt Me Titi • 1 Fromage Blanc • 1 spring water • 2milks,
1 Beer • tin dog • cake lunch, 1 castersugar • 1 Powdered chocolate
Lemon • Staples • Photocopy • Meat this evening

Adeline

I'm off to pick Titi up from nursery, and then we'll go for a little picnic in the park. My sweetheart, my little pussy cat. He's so cute, I'm so proud of him. You have to admit he's so much more advanced than the other kids of his age. You'd think they were autistic – they're barely talking, whereas he's already forming his words properly. My Titi. My little pussy cat. When he grows up, he'll be a lawyer.

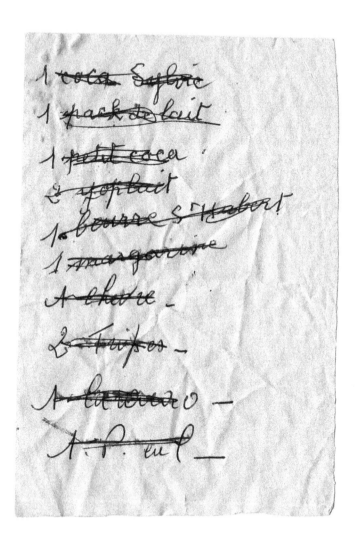

1 cola Sylvie • 1 pack of milk • 1 little cola • 2 yoplait • 1 butter
St Hubert • 1 margarine • 1 goat • 2 Tripe • 1 larouao • 1 P. toil

Josette

You can say what you like. Claude's no doctor though. He says to me, 'Dairy products make your ears itch, just there, inside'. And he's not wrong! For instance, just the other day, with the strawberries – cos Laurent and Sylvie had come for tea – with the strawberries, I'd prepared some fromage blanc. With sugar. Obviously, I didn't want any but, of course, when everyone had finished eating, there was still some left. Pierrot didn't want any more, and Claude said he was full – I'd cooked up some tripe, see – and anyway fromage blanc don't keep well in the fridge. So, like an idiot, I ended up eating the lot. And sure as eggs is eggs ... All night long, my ears were itching! Claude was right. Even though he's no doctor.

10 coquille St Jacques
500 g girolles
1 br celeri
3 ~~echalotes~~
2 ~~gousses ail~~
Ciboulette - Cerfeuil
5 tr saumon 2,5 cm Ep
500 g pate feulletée
250 g crevettes décortiqués
estragon
citron
crème fraiche
caramel
crème patissière
choc noir

10 scallops • 500 g girolle mushrooms • 1 st celery • ~~3 spring onions~~
~~3 bulbs garlic~~ • chives • chervil • 5 sl sammon 2.5cm Thk • 500 g
flaky pastry • 250 g peeled shrimp • tarragon • lemon
créle fraiche • caramel • pastry cream • dark choc

Kelly

This time, you might say I've pulled out all the stops. It's gonna be better than that *Come Dine with Me* on the telly. A right old spread, going all out. I had a look through the online recipes on the Marmiton site, where they explain everything, and it all looks just about doable. Okay, for the flaky pastry, I'm getting ready-made – no need to go over the top. And anyway, I don't reckon you can tell the difference. It'll wow the hell out of them, and then they'll have to admit that I know how to cook, no question. Where there's a will, there's a way, that's what I always say. I just hope I don't cock it all up and no one falls ill, like they did last time.

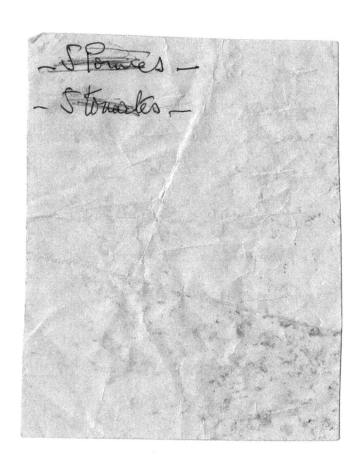

5 Apples • 5 tomatoes

Anis

I remember exactly the day I stopped believing in God. I was six years old. The cat had gone missing, and I prayed for him to come back safe and sound, because he was a nice cat, and because it wouldn't be fair if anything happened to him. The next day, he was found dead by the side of the road. He'd been hit by a car. He wasn't all squashed or anything – there was just a tiny drop of blood running from his nose. That was when I said to myself that if God couldn't answer such a simple prayer, either he didn't exist, or he was rubbish at his job and didn't deserve to have people believe in him.

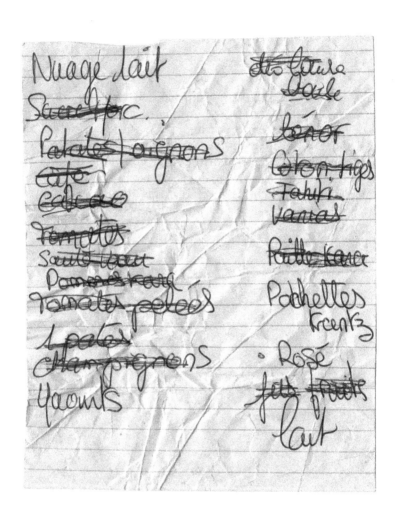

Evaporated milk • ~~Sugar cub~~ • ~~Spuds/onions~~ • coffee • coco • ~~Tomatoes~~
~~veal sauté~~ • ~~Peeled tomatoes~~ • ~~1 pasta~~ • mushrooms • yoghurts
~~Laure deodorant~~ • ~~roll-on~~ • lenor • ~~cotton buds~~ • ~~Tahiti~~ • vanila • ~~Kara straw~~
Krcentz Plastic pockets • Rosé • ~~Fruit juice~~ • milk

Ludovic

In the morning, when I wake up, it's as if I were coming out of a coma. I'm no use to anyone, for three hours at least. Often, I can't remember where I am, and it'll take me a while to get my bearings in my head. Sometimes, I think I'm still waking up in the bedroom I had as a kid, living with my parents, with the wall to the right side of the bed and the window to the left. Then I get all confused. But this morning, when I opened my eyes, I looked at my arm and I didn't know what it was. I looked at this inert mass lying next to me, and I wondered to myself who it belonged to and what it did. I didn't even know who I was. Luckily, after a while, I managed to remember.

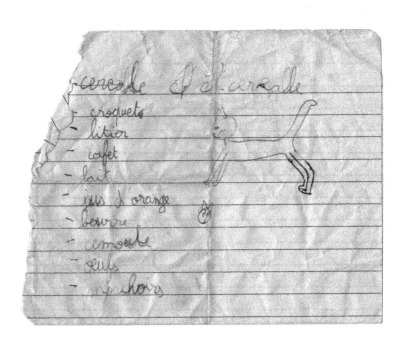

sereal • *cl cl* • *sereal* • *kible* • *cat litter* • *cofee* • *milk* • *juice*
orange • *butter* • *semalina* • *eggs* • *tissues*

Noé

Today, my friend Reda told me his grandad died this weekend. He didn't really wanna talk about it, he just came out with it, like that, when it was just us two, away from the others in the playground. He said: 'I feel really down, man. I really, really loved my grandad'. So I said to him that I understand if he felt down, cos I'd feel really down if my grandma died. But then after that, it was a bit awkward cos I couldn't really think of anything else I should say to him … It's the first time I've had to console a friend for that – it was weird. So we went to play with the others.

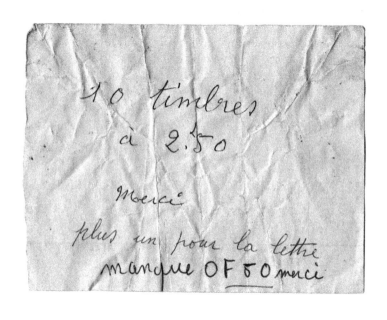

10 stamps at 2'50 • thanks • plus one for the letter • short OF50
thanks

Denise

My, what a day! The bus was supposed to be there at 3:00 p.m. 3:00 p.m. is what it said in black and white on the timetables. I checked. Well, I got to the stop a good ten minutes early, around 2:52. And I waited. Nothing. At five past, when it should have been there at least five minutes earlier, not a bus in sight. At a quarter past, still nothing! I wondered if there'd been an accident, if it had been delayed or something, but I had no way of knowing. Half an hour I had to wait. Out in the sun and with nowhere to sit. When the next bus finally came along – the 3:28 – I made a point of asking the driver. But he couldn't give me an answer. I'd have liked to have gotten to the bottom of it, and find out why the 3 o'clock bus hadn't turned up. But he didn't know. All he could say was, 'We don't know other drivers' timetables, just our own'. Even so! And yet I'd checked: 3:00 p.m., that's what it said in black and white. Next time, just in case, I'll take my collapsible umbrella with me.

1 Naunours
1 Crocodiles
2 Cacahouette
2 Blanc

1 Teddy Bear • 1 Crocodiles • 2 Peanuts • 2 White

Katia

He truly is what you'd call an artist, that one. No sense of the realities of life. Anyone can spend their time coming up with little Mickey Mouse drawings. Easy. But in the real world, that ain't how it works. This ain't Care Bear land or something – he's gonna have to snap out of it. There are papers to sort, school meals to pay for, and the car needs taking to the garage – seems like he's not interested in any of that. I've got a real job, and I work my arse off for next to nothing. Whereas he gets paid for sitting around and doing his drawings in the warm. For him, everything simply lands gift-wrapped in his lap. It's crap.

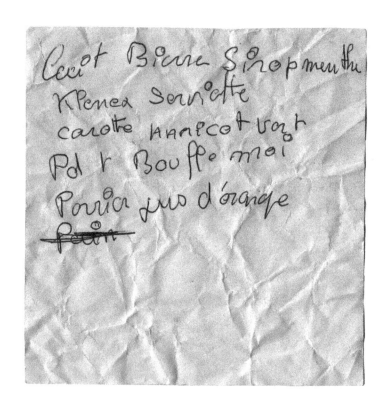

milk • Beer • Mint cordial • Klenex • serviettes • carrot • green been
Spuds Grub me • Perrier • orange juice • ~~Bread~~

Bruno

Christiane is never gonna get over this one. 3,000 euros paid straight into our account. It's from some charity, Social Services Support for All. Never heard of them. It's awesome. The woman on the phone explained they'd picked our name randomly from the phone book. But in order to receive the cash, you had to confirm by phoning a free number. I called it, but I just heard a beep and then it hung up. 3,000 euros – that's a lot of money. With that, we could eat out at a restaurant at least two hundred times, or fill the car with petrol sixty times. We could even go on holiday, or I don't know what else we could do with it – just thinking about it makes me giddy. She's gonna be blown away, she is, when I tell her about this.

Pig's liver or white pudding • ~~Delacre biscuits~~ (2 packets) (Namur)
1 ~~breaded pig's trotter~~ • 1 [rabbit carousel • Yoplait Yellow Fruit
Yohgerts • Rice pudding dairy long-life • 1 ~~Coffee l'Or Absolu~~..%..

Sylviane

The sun cast its dying rays over the horizon ablaze with a riot of purple-pink hues, and the immense ocean poured the filigree froth of its waves onto the sand, still warm. Out to sea, white sails drifted away into the distance. It was dusk, heralding the end of another superb day – as they so often are in Santa Monica. Beth and Lorenzo walked along the shingle beach without saying a single word. The light reflecting on the waves danced on Lorenzo's bare, bronze-toned skin, and made Beth's mane of untamed gold sparkle with a wild glow. Suddenly, Lorenzo stopped in his tracks. His handsome face looked solemn, as if troubled by some deep inner turmoil. 'Oh, Beth ...', he murmured. Overcome by some undefinable *frisson*, she turned to face him, and guessed the terrible confession that did not dare leave his finely drawn lips. The ardour of his desire made her quiver. But it was too late. She knew it. And the last bastion of her trepidation was swept away by the power of their love. She closed her eyes and abandoned herself entirely to passion as their lips touched and locked together at last. Beth was embracing the first happy minute of her life, in the arms of the man whom – until that moment – she had so feared. 'I am lost', she uttered with a sigh of ecstasy. And bang. That's how it ends. I can't wait for Marie-France to finish the one after so she can lend it me. I reckon that Lorenzo guy's a bit dodgy – he's not right for her. The poor girl – what with everything she's been through. My God, really – it'll all end in tears, I'm telling you.

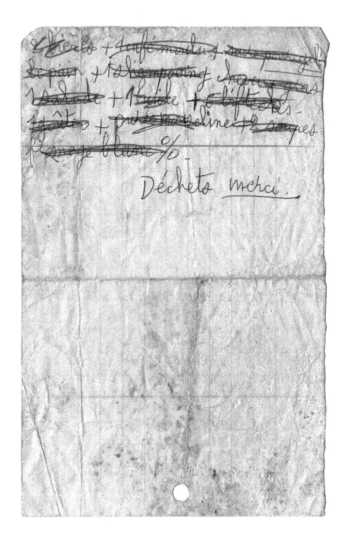

2 beers + 1 ground coffee + sugar for jelly • the bread + 1 shampoo greasy hair • 1 salad + 1 oil + 6 steaks • 1 snack + 1 mash mouseline + 2 soups • fromage blanc % • Bins <u>thanks.</u>

Gregory

Of course the elite are frightened by what we've found out. They do everything they can to make sure the public know nothing of the truth. They want to force us back into line, like nice, docile puppets, and get rid of any obstacles so they can happily instigate World War Four, making the most of biological warfare and artificial intelligence. And they do all that so they can launder their worldwide scams and serve the interests of the invisible finance groups who are manipulating us. The industrial pressure groups behind them want to keep their monopoly, with the complicity of the leading class. The brainwashing of the masses has been a success, so when these embarrassing revelations come out, people would rather stick their head in the sand. And those who know tend to keep their mouth shut – they're too scared of reprisals. The enemy is strong. There are quite a few people who've lost everything through asking too many questions. Their kids get taken while they're asleep, others just happen to die from some mystery disease, or their pets go missing or are replaced by fakes. That's how they kick any rumblings into touch. But they're not fooling anyone. What they want is to bring the Apocalypse down on us.

démaquillant.
400 G de chocolat ~~nestelle~~ nestlé
6 oeufs est de la grenadine

make–up remover • 400 G of chocolate ~~nestelle~~ nestlé
6 eggs an pomegranate squash

Mégane

I can't stand living with my parents anymore. I've totally got to find a job. But things are so tough. The economical situation stinks, and if you've not got the right qualifications, there's no chance anyone'll take you on. Nowadays, even doctors are working as cashiers cos things are so bad. So, with my qualifications, I can't even imagine what my options are. I'm gonna have to marry a man who's rich and who'll want me to give him five kids, just because I'm so rubbish and so stupid and so dyslexic.

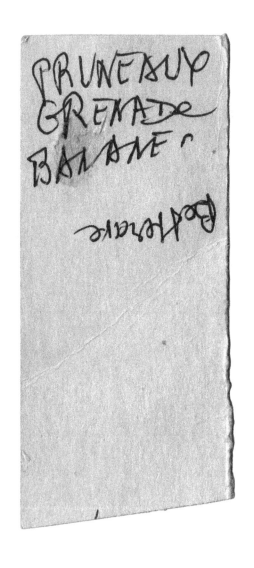

PRUNES • POMEGRANATE • BANANA
Beetroot

Sébastien

Earlier, on the bus, it was packed – like it always is during lunch break. There was this young hipster guy who started having a go at the dude sitting next to him cos he'd supposedly trodden on his foot or something, but all he was trying to do, he said, was squish up to let people get past. Then he spotted a seat that had just been freed and he shot to it like a leopard. On my way back, going past the Gare Saint-Lazare, what should I happen to see but his ugly mug. He was having a right set-to with some other bloke who looked like he had him by the collar. Serves the sod right.

Yaourts 0%.
Yaourts pour mon AMOUR
whiskas pour nos puces
litière
Pains au chocolat
Pain de son
Steacks hachés minimum 6
Escalopes
Jambon
Thon
Pommes pas chères pour compote
sinon compote en boîte sans sucre
Pommes de terre
Poisson surgelé.
Petit pot crème fraîche
citrons (2 ou 3)
jus pamplemousse.

*Yoghurts 0% • Yoghurts for my LOVE • whiskas for our darlings
cat litter • Pains au chocolat • Bran bread • ham burgers minimum 6
Escalopes • Ham • Tuna • Cheap apples to make compote if not
tinned compote <u>sugar free</u> • Potatoes • Frozen fish • Little
pot crème fraiche • lemons (2 or 3) • grapefruit juice*

Angélique

I know, my poor darlings, we're sad because Daddy's not here, I know, we're sad, and Mummy's sad too, and she wishes Daddy were already back home from work. Three times I've called him, but it keeps going to voice mail. My poor love, he must still be stuck in some meeting. I know. I know, my darlings. Daddy works too much. All this week, he's got back after 8 p.m., and he doesn't have time to give you cuddles any more. You're good cats, you are. You're good cats with your paws and your ears. Daddy will be home soon. He's working to buy you lovely Whiskas, my sweethearts. But he's promised me that next weekend, we'll all be together. Now, now, stop being naughty, and come and give Mummy a kiss, instead of scratching the sofa.

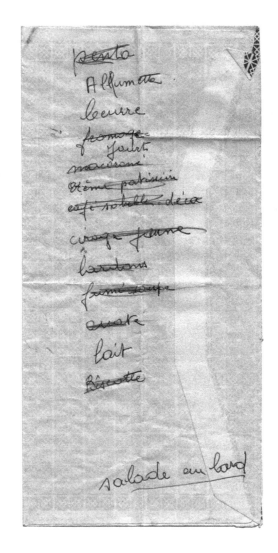

pento • Matches • butter • cheese • yurts • macaroni
pastry cream • instant coffee decaf • dubbin • smoked
lardons soup • cotton wool • milk • Crispbread • bacon salad

Alfredo

As Serge Reggiani used to sing, 'For a child as old as me, life on
the road gets weary'. But I have to say that when I got to this
village, the emotion was so ... it was so ... I thought to myself,
this is where my parents lived, this is where they fell in love, this
is where I was born. And to think I'd never known these parts,
this country. And it seemed so beautiful to me, Italy, so beautiful,
that since then I've felt a bit Italian. *I* am the Italian Serge sang
about ... 'Is there anyone in, man or woman, are you theeere? Open
up, open the door, and let me iiin!' Okay, so now I'm singing out
loud ... What will people think? Dear me, Alfredo, you're losing
your marbles.

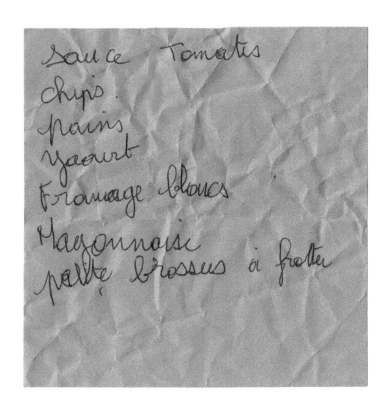

Sauce • Tomatoes • crisps • bread • yoghurt • Fromage blancs
Mayonnaise • little scrubbing brushes

Éric

When I go, I want to be buried in a squatting position, so when the Last Judgement comes, I can be first to leap out.

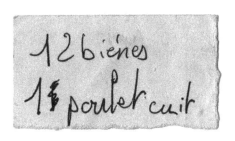

12 beers • 1 ½ cooked chicken

Lionel

It turns out they're saying the weather's going to be lovely, and I can't wait. Last year, we had a bit of rain in the morning, but then it cleared up, and it got as hot as in summer. Fabrice had dug a hole in the ground to keep his beers cool – something he supposedly learnt from a Vietnam veteran. But – no offence intended – I still think a cool box is better. We got the deckchairs out, and chilled for the whole of the afternoon, doing sod all. Towards the evening, it got cold all of a sudden, and with it came the damp. We put jumpers on and stayed outside all the same. There wasn't a cloud in the sky, and in the dark the stars were really bright, as if they were really close – not like in the city, where everything's half-orange. Just like that, for a laugh, I started coming out with a few names I'd heard in some documentary. Like, so that's Ursa Major, that's Orion, that one's Andromeda, and the speck you can see over there is Cassiopeia. That won me some points, coming over as some sort of expert – they couldn't bloody believe it. But even so, I ended up telling them I was just messing around. Later, the ladies got a bit stressed because of the bats, cos of course in films they cling to your hair and suck your blood like vampires. Us blokes told them that was a load of rubbish, but – you have to admit – it's true that having those things flying around can freak you out. Then the next day, we got up late and did sod all again, but we had to leave early to avoid the traffic. It was a bit sad, having to say goodbye to everyone so early. We'd have liked to have stayed for longer, but we had no choice – had to be back for work on Monday, and money doesn't grow on trees. On the way home, as usual, we stank of smoke from the fire, our mouths were as dry as a witch's teat, and our faces were burned cos we'd caught the sun. It was bloody brilliant.

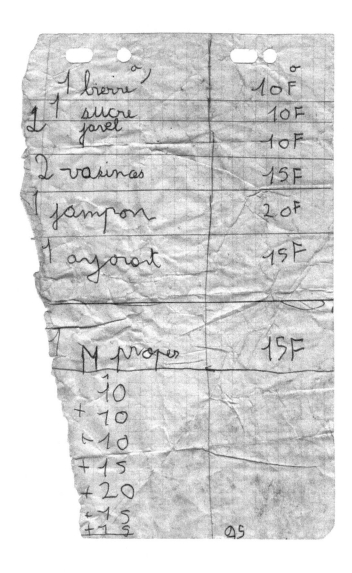

1 beer 10 F • 1 sugar 10 F • 2 bleach 10 F • 2 mops 15 F
1 ham 20 F • 1 yohgurt 15 F • 1 Mr Clean 15 F
10 + 10 + 10 + 15 +20 +15 + 15 / 95

Louise

If I had to choose, for when I'm older, I'd be a vet. I'll open a hospital in New York, and it'll have all the specialists you need to look after animals, and there'll be an equestrian centre, too. Also, we'll take in any wild animals or birds injured in the forest, and we'll look after them. I'll live with Izia, who'll still be my best friend forever. She's going to be a make-up artist to celebs. That or an interior designer. And also, I'll act in films. I'll have time to do it, cos I'll run my own company.

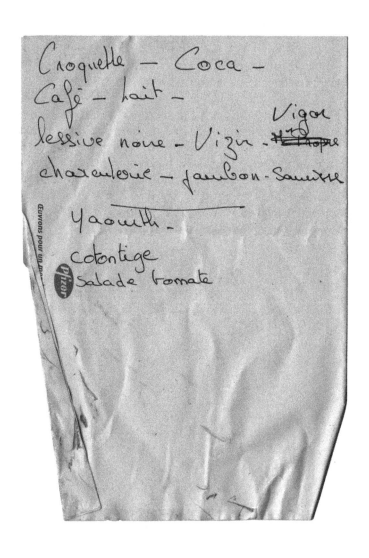

Croquette • Coca • Coffee • Milk • dark washing powder • Vizir • Mr Clean Vigor
cold meats • ham • sausage • yogurth • cottonbud • tomato salad

Adel

There are places in the countryside where nobody locks anything up – they just go off and do their shopping and leave their front door wide open. They leave their car unlocked as well. Since I had my sat-nav stolen, I'm always nervous. At home, I have to check everything three times, to make sure it's all properly locked. I go round the house, checking each lock in the same order – I find it reassuring. When it's done, I feel better. I'm well aware that it's not rational, but if I don't do it, the thought of it will be stuck in my head, and it makes me anxious. It's tiring, always having to do the same thing over and over again, but if I didn't, I'd have no peace of mind. What I should do – it would help – is maybe do some research into different types of alarms, have a look at them, do some comparisons, just to be sure.

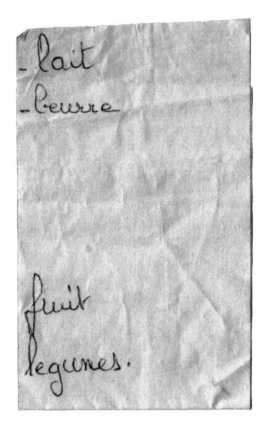

milk • butter
fruit • vegetables

Philippe

At work, during the break, me and a few of the guys were having a chat. We were talking about women celebs we found beautiful. To begin with, we were coming out with the names of actresses, and then I thought of James Franco, y'know, the one who plays Spider-Man's mate. He's so hot. Fournier turned on me like a shot. He said that, as a bloke, he couldn't possibly have an opinion on how good-looking a man was, that the whole subject didn't concern him, and that he had no more to say on the matter. I tried telling him that, obviously, beauty is something subjective, but he could at least form an opinion based on criteria defined by most people, and that having an opinion about this did not put in doubt either his virility or his heterosexuality. But the conversation just ended there. He was upset. It makes me wonder how he looks at people. When he sees a man, does everything become all blurred and vague, but if it's a woman he's looking at, everything's clear? Anyway, since same-sex marriage was legalised, he won't even say 'hello' to me. He told me, frankly, that I could do what I wanted with my life, but that marriage between two men, no – end of. It's turned out quite well, really, cos I had no intention of asking him to marry me. Fournier looks nothing like James Franco. Not even vaguely.

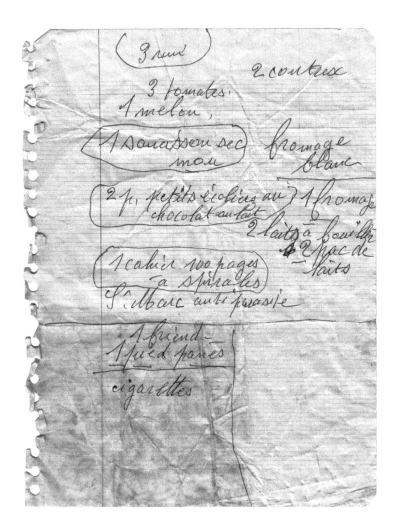

3 mir • 2 contrex • 3 tomatoes • 1 melon • 1 soft dry saucisson
fromage blanc • 2 p. milk chocolate petits écoliers • 1 cheese
2 milks to boil • ̶1̶ 2 pacs of milk • 1 spiral notebook 100 pages
St Marc anti parasite • 1 friend • 1 breaded trotters • cigarettes

Carole

What a load of sheep. They're not interested in anything, they can't remember anything. All they can think about is liking photos of cats on Facebook, or texting 'Yo wassup' to each other on the sly. This – it would seem – is what characterises Gen Z, force-fed at the teat of social media and the new media world. Generation Z for 'zooming', indeed. They can't even look up the meaning of a word in a dictionary, they can't spell, they've zero perseverance, and about as much ability to concentrate as a goldfish. But when it comes to the names of people on TV, well, they know them by heart, no problem. When I think that tomorrow I've been lumbered with the lesson on the Battle of Verdun, it makes me sick to my stomach. And I'll have to find some angle to make it sexy and fun, somehow. So, General von Falkenhayn was like totally pissed off and decided to have a go at the French troops. Pétain totally owned the guy, but all the same there were 700,000 dead, which is equivalent to the population of Detroit, in the US – the city where the singer Eminem started out. Sheesh! Four hours of being thrown to the lions ... and the first day back at school after the summer to boot. Great. But oh yes, of course, what am I complaining about? We get too many holidays and other people's taxes pay us to sit around doing nothing. I'm always forgetting just how lucky I am.

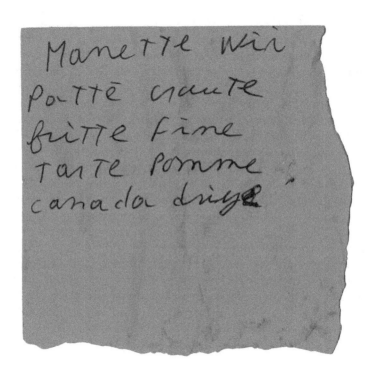

Wii controller • patté croute • skinny fries • Apple Tart • Canada drie

Corentin

Space: 1999! They fight each other with staple guns, and they're dressed in beige pyjamas. It's brilliant. There's this research centre on the moon, and there's an accident that sends the moon shooting off into space. From an astronomical point of view, it's pretty unlikely. On their different missions, they encounter space creatures – usually women wearing togas and too much make-up – with names like Saha, Maya, or Shahana. The special effects they use must've cost a packet, for a TV series back then, but they're a bit crap. I love it!

Wine • Tongue • bread • Meat

Youri

She's always got something to say – it never stops. She talks and she talks – it's all she can do. She tells me how her day's gone, then she tells me the news of the people she's bumped into in the morning, then she tells me what she's heard on the radio or seen on TV, talks about the day's weather or what the weather will be like tomorrow, reads the newspaper out loud to me, and repeats – in great detail – all the news she's heard at the market. When she's not doing that, she sings. I can never find anything to say back. So she talks and she talks – she talks to make me feel bad for not saying anything.

Cuisses poulet
Blanquette veau
chipo — escalope dinde
Jambon
Rillettes
Cotes d'agneau doubles
bananes — Nouille riz
Fromage -beurre -
eaux
crème
oeufs
petits pois carotte
Ravioli - cassoulet
Sauce Spagheli Bolognaise

Chicken thighs • Veal stew • chipo • turkey escalopes • ham
Potted meat • double lamb chops • bananas • Noodles • rice • Cheese
butter • water • cream • eggs • peas carrots • Ravioli • cassoulet
spagheli Bolognaise sauce

Daniel

I'm gonna stop mucking around – from now on, I'm gonna be careful. I've already given up the booze. Well, except for wine, cos you can't count that as alcohol. And I've almost completely given up fatty foods, and I've quit smoking – apart from one cigar a day. I went back to see the surgeon who did my double bypass operation at Pitié-Salpêtrière Hospital. Those chaps work their socks off. It's different to labouring, like being a roofer or a builder, but even so … they work their socks off. If only out of respect for what they do, I've decided to be careful and not die any time soon.

Underpants • cat • water

Maxime

It's better to be alone than in a bad relationship, that's obvious. There's plenty more fish in the sea. Now, at least, I can do what I want, when I want. I don't have to sit at the table to eat, and there's nobody telling me what to do or having a go at me for leaving my undercrackers lying around. I'm chill. I can listen to my own music again, and choose what film I want to watch. If I wanted, I could wear the same T-shirt all week long. It's the best. This is happiness. This is freedom. If I feel like hanging out with my mates, I just go and see them, whenever I want – and now there's no risk of narky comments. Seriously, I'm more than happy on my own. I'm never bored and I totally have no regrets. In fact, I wish the new guy Good Luck.

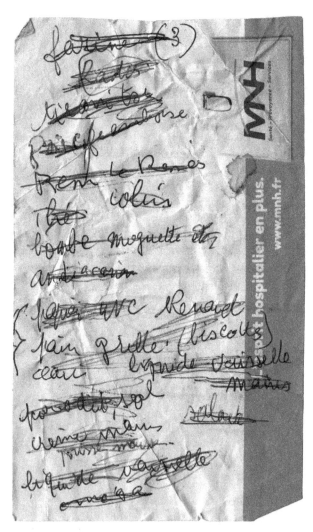

flour (3) • Radish • tiramitsu • Punnet raspberries • REM Le Renés • Tea
coley • summer carpit freshener • dust mite stopper • Renaud toilet paper • melba
toast • water • (biscottes) • washing–up liquid hands • floor cleaner • hand
cream dispenser • salad • washing–up liquid • omega

Serge

It's funny. I've seen how fashion's changed since I was a kid. Thirty-five years ago, hair was still all over the place. Armpit hair was first to go. Then shaving around the genitals came in, and that turned into complete pubic hair removal, especially among young female patients. Occasionally, in films supposedly set in the nineteenth century, you can spot the odd anachronism in that you'll see women with no body hair whatsoever. That makes no sense. If Gustave Courbet were alive today, his painting *The Origin of the World* would be completely different. But it's not our problem – at least, not yet. Maybe one day. In the meantime, the wife's at the beautician's and I have to sort the shopping out. I'll have to get a move on, if I want to be there when the surgery opens.

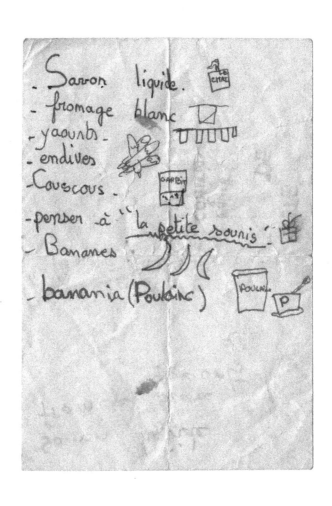

Handwash • fromage blanc • yoghurts • endives • Couscous
think about 'the tooth fairy' • Bananas • banania (Poulainc)

Clémentine

This morning, when the bell rang, the others ran outside, pushing and shoving and shouting. I don't enjoy going to play outside. Just running around for no reason, playing stupid games, it's not fun for me. It's better being in the quiet and being able to think calmly about things and doing drawings. So, I asked Miss Salabay if I could stay inside, and she was fine with it. I could hear the noise coming from the playground, I watched the clouds through the window, and Miss gave me a fruit jelly. It was the most beautiful playtime of my life.